How to Talk to Anyone

7 Communication Secrets to Effortlessly Break the Ice, Become the Most Interesting Person in the Room, and Build Genuine Relationships

Rowan Beckett

Table of Contents

Introduction 7

Before Moving Forward, Let's Expand on What is the Effective Communication 8

Keep Reading Until the End of the Book, and We Will Achieve the Goal! 10

Chapter 1: Fundamentals of Communication 11

Understanding Communication Models 12

The Role of Listening 21

Verbal vs Non-Verbal Communication 22

Communication Barriers 27

Chapter 2: Listening Mastery 36

Active Listening Techniques 37

Empathic Listening 41

Overcoming Listening Biases and Selective Hearing 44

Listening in the Digital Age 47

Chapter 3: Speak with Confidence 50

Articulate Thoughts Clearly 51

Tips for Public Speaking 53

Overcome Fear and Anxiety 62

Storytelling as a Tool 67

Chapter 4: The Nuances of Body Language............ 70

Deciphering Gestures and Postures....................70

The Impact of Facial Expressions 77

Understanding Proxemics........................... 80

Cultural Differences in Body Language 82

Chapter 5: Creating Connections......................... 85

The Art of Casual Chat..................................85

Building Connection Speed......................... 90

Networking Strategies..................................92

Deepening Personal Relationships 94

Chapter 6: Advanced Communication Skills........... 97

Persuasive Communication.........................97

Negotiation Tactics 100

Conflict Management 104

Communication Across Cultures...................105

Chapter 7: Special Communication Contexts.........107

Professional Communication 108

Social Networks and Online Communication 110

Intercultural Communication 112

Family and Intimate Communication 114

Chapter 8: Overcoming Common Challenges 117

Dealing with Difficult People 117

Communicating Under Pressure........................ *119*

Adapting to Changing Environments...........................*120*

Overcoming Misunderstandings........................*122*

Chapter 9: Practical Application and Exercises...... 124

Daily Communication Practices........................*124*

Role-Playing Scenarios.....................................*131*

Feedback and Continuous Improvement..........................*133*

Building a Personal Communication Plan *134*

Chapter 10: Development of Communication Throughout Life.. 136

Establishing and Achieving Communication Objectives .*136*

The Role of Mentoring and Coaching *137*

Join Communication Groups and Communities *138*

Embracing Continuous Learning........................*139*

Conclusion... 142

HERE'S THE AWARD YOU DESERVE

Here's what you'll find inside:

- **1. MASTER PERSUASION:** Turn every conversation into an opportunity by strengthening both personal and professional relationships.
- **2. CONFLICTS? NO PROBLEM:** Leverage calmness and collaboration to transform challenges and difficult individuals into shared successes.
- **3. FROM START TO FINISH:** Learn to set up, negotiate, and successfully close, managing each stage with expertise.

SCAN HERE TO DOWNLOAD IT

Introduction

Welcome to this space dedicated to transforming the way you communicate with the world. You are about to embark on a process that will equip you with excellent communication skills that will enable you to interact confidently and effectively in any context.

Effective communication is crucial for building meaningful relationships, resolving conflicts, and advancing your professional career.

Imagine for a moment an ordinary day in which simple misunderstandings escalate into unnecessary arguments, where your intentions are misinterpreted, generating tension and distance. This scenario, which may seem exaggerated, is an everyday reality for many people. Lack of clarity, not actively listening, or misinterpreting non-verbal tone can lead to conflicts that, in many cases, could be completely avoided.

Now, visualize a change in that scenario: your words flow in a way that every person around you understands what you say, what you feel, and what you think. Conflicts are easily resolved because you can express your ideas clearly and empathetically, listening and responding to the concerns of others so that you build bridges instead of walls. This change is more than possible; it is achievable with the practice and application of the principles you will find in this book.

Effective communication has the power to transform your life completely. For example, in a professional environment, consider the difference between a presentation that grabs everyone's attention, persuades, and motivates, and one that is forgotten by the end of the presentation. The first can open doors, connect you to opportunities, and establish you as a leader in your field. On a personal level, imagine the ability to forge deep and meaningful connections, where you feel you are understood and valued. The difference is in how you communicate.

Before Moving Forward, Let's Expand on What is the Effective Communication

Effective communication is presented as a bridge between individuals, allowing the exchange of ideas, thoughts, emotions, and values in a clear and understandable way. But what makes communication effective and why is it so important in our lives?

In its essence, this communication occurs when the sender and the receiver of a message achieve a common understanding, where intentions and feelings are understood as they were intended. This involves transmitting a message clearly and precisely, and actively listening—the latter is a skill that requires full attention and empathy toward the other's perspective. This two-way process ensures that a deeper connection is built between people.

The importance of effective communication is that it affects almost every aspect of our lives.

Furthermore, we live in a globalized era where interactions often transcend cultural and geographical borders. In this context, the ability to communicate effectively with people from different cultures is essential, allowing us to overcome cultural barriers.

To achieve this level of communication, we must resort to the conscious practice of skills that I have already mentioned, and that I will expand on throughout the chapters of this book, such as active listening, clarity of expression, empathy, and adaptation to the interlocutor's non-verbal language. It also implies the ability to adapt to different contexts and audiences, choosing the most appropriate tone, style, and medium for each situation.

Imagine being able to express your ideas with confidence and clarity, feel heard and understood in your relationships, and navigate conflict with grace and effectiveness— this is the power of effective communication: it transforms how we interact with the world and how the world responds to us. Therefore, more than a simple skill, it is a fundamental pillar for success and satisfaction in life, it invites you to look beyond words and understand the importance of how we use them. By mastering this art, you improve your ability to interact with others and open the door to a deeper understanding of yourself and the world around you.

Keep Reading Until the End of the Book, and We Will Achieve the Goal!

This book is designed to be your guide through this transformation process. From understanding the fundamentals of communication to mastering advanced skills, I will offer you a blend of theory and practice that will make learning accessible and relevant. Each chapter builds on the previous one, ensuring you have a solid foundation before moving on to more complex concepts.

For this knowledge to be translated into real change, I invite you to adopt a practical attitude; beyond understanding the concepts, I encourage you to apply them in your daily life. Try active listening techniques in your conversations, observe body language in your interactions, and experiment with different ways of expressing your ideas.

This is the first step towards a new way of interacting with those around you, marked by understanding, empathy, and trust.

Chapter 1: Fundamentals of Communication

Now that you have started reading this book, it is time to lay the foundations with the first chapter: Communication Fundamentals.

Starting with the fundamentals gives you the necessary structure to understand the more complex aspects of communication that we will explore later. Think of these fundamentals as the foundation of a house; without a solid foundation, any structure you build on top of it could be unstable and eventually collapse.

By the end of this chapter, you will have gained a solid understanding of why communicating effectively is so important in all areas of our lives, this foundation will allow you to move toward more advanced communication techniques and strategies with the confidence that you are building on solid ground. The benefits of having solid foundations in communication are countless: from improving your personal and professional relationships to increasing your ability to influence and persuade others, they offer you the advantage of being able to navigate the complex world of human interaction with greater ease and effectiveness. Therefore, the goal of this chapter is not simply to provide you with information, it is to transform the way you think and act in your daily interactions. You will become a better listener, a clearer communicator, and ultimately someone capable of building deeper, more meaningful connections.

Therefore, I invite you to approach this chapter with an open mind and a commitment to apply what you learn. This is the first step towards developing a communicative competence that will accompany you in all facets of your life, opening doors to new opportunities and improving your relationships in a deep and lasting way.

Understanding Communication Models

Communication models are theoretical schemes that describe how messages are transmitted between senders and receivers; they serve as conceptual maps to understand the various components and processes involved in communication. By studying them, you gain a more structured view of how communication is carried out and why certain interactions are more successful than others, allowing you to identify and improve areas of your communication that may not be working as well as they could.

Each model highlights different aspects of communication, from the simplicity of the exchange of messages to the complexity of the contexts and perceptions that affect the interpretation of those messages.

So, keep reading and learn the details of each of them:

1. Linear Communication Model

Under this model, communication is presented as a unidirectional process where the sender sends a message to the receiver without waiting for a response. An everyday example would be when you listen to the radio. The speaker (sender) shares news or music (message) through the radio (channel), reaching listeners (receivers) without the latter providing direct feedback to the speaker.

Key aspects of the linear communication model:

- **Single sender initiates communication:** A single person or entity is responsible for generating and sending the message.

- **Clear and concise message to avoid misunderstandings:** The message must be direct and easy to understand, considering that there will be no immediate opportunity for clarification.

- **Defined channel as a transmission medium:** The medium through which the message is sent, such as radio, television, or print media, plays a crucial role in the effective delivery of the message.

- **Passive receiver without active participation:** The target person or group receives the message without interacting with the sender or influencing the content of the message.

- **No feedback from the receiver to the sender:** There is no mechanism for the receiver to respond directly to the received message.

- **Simple context without the need for deep interpretation:** The message is delivered in an environment that requires little interpretation on the part of the receiver.

- **Minimum influence of noise on message transmission:** It is assumed that there are few distractions or interference that could disturb the clear reception of the message.

- **Limited effectiveness for interaction and commitment:** This model does not encourage a two-way relationship or the commitment of the recipient.

- **Unidirectionality characterizes the communication flow:** The message flows in only one direction, from the sender to the receiver.

- **Predominance in mass media:** Ideal for situations where the same message needs to be sent to many people.

- **Does not consider varied or subjective interpretations of the message:** The model does not address how different individuals can interpret the message differently.

- **Easy to understand and apply in appropriate contexts:** Due to its simplicity, it is easily applicable in situations that do not require interaction.

Although this model offers a foundation for understanding communication in its most basic form, its suitability is limited in contexts that require interactivity, feedback, and adaptation of the message based on the recipient's response.

Its application is most effective in situations where information needs to be distributed quickly and widely without the need for direct interaction, such as in public announcements or news broadcasts.

In environments where mutual understanding and dialogue are decisive, this model falls short, since it does not allow the message to be adjusted based on the feedback or reactions of the recipient, limiting its usefulness in deep and meaningful interpersonal communication.

2. Interactive Communication Model

This model adds an element absent in the linear model: feedback.

Interactive model considers communication as a two-way process, where both the sender and the receiver exchange roles, and there is a constant interaction through feedback. For example, a Q&A session at a conference, where the speaker presents information and attendees respond or ask questions, creates a flow of communication in both directions.

The key aspects of this communication model are:

- **Exchange of roles between sender and receiver:** Both participants in the communication alternate their roles, going from being senders to receivers and vice versa.

- **Feedback as the central axis of the process:** Feedback allows the message to be adjusted and refined in real-time, improving mutual understanding.

- **Bidirectional communication channels:** Messages are not only sent but also received through the same channel, allowing continuous interaction.

- **Incorporation of noise and barriers in interpretation:** This model recognizes that external and internal factors can affect the clarity of the message and the effectiveness of communication.

- **Dynamic contexts and situations influence communication:** The situation or environment in which communication takes place affects the process and interpretation of messages.

- **Use of non-verbal signals to reinforce the message:** Gestures, facial expressions, and tone of voice complement the verbal message, enriching communication.

- **Feedback allows adaptation and adjustment of the message:** Based on the receiver's response, the sender can modify their communication to improve understanding.

- **Interaction in real-time or delayed:** Although ideally it is immediate, feedback can also occur after some time, especially in digital media.

- **Relevance of perception and interpretation:** How each participant interprets the message can change the course of the communication.

- **Facilitates relationship building and mutual understanding:** By allowing exchange, a greater connection is encouraged between participants.

- **It implies greater participation and commitment of the interlocutors:** The need to respond or give feedback implies active participation.

- **Requires active listening skills and adaptability:** To be effective, participants must be able to correctly interpret feedback and adjust their communication accordingly.

The interactive communication model is highly convenient in contexts where interaction and the exchange of ideas are fundamental; it provides a more realistic and dynamic framework for communication, recognizing the importance of feedback in the process.

Allowing adjustments in the message based on the recipient's response facilitates better understanding and can help overcome communication barriers, although it may be less effective in situations where time is limited or when information is required to be transmitted to many people simultaneously without the possibility of individual interaction.

3. Transactional Communication Model

This model represents communication as a dynamic and simultaneous process in which all parties involved are both senders and receivers at the same time, emphasizing the interdependence of the participants and how each one affects and is affected by the communication. A practical example of this model is observed in a conversation between friends, where expressions, emotions, and reactions are shared and perceived in real time, influencing the course of the conversation in a continuous and fluid way.

Regarding its key aspects, they are:

- **Simultaneity in the exchange of roles:** The participants in the communication act as senders and receivers at the same time, creating a continuous flow of information.

- **Interdependence of participants:** Each person in the communication process influences and is influenced by the others, creating a dynamic environment of interaction.

- **Feedback integrated into communication:** Feedback is instantaneous and is an intrinsic part of the exchange, not as a later addition.

- **Importance of non-verbal and contextual cues:** Gestures, facial expressions, tone of voice, and the environment play a crucial role in the interpretation of messages.

- **The context influences the interpretation of the message:** The situation or environment in which communication occurs modifies the way how messages are understood and expressed.

- **Co-creation of meaning:** The participants collaborate in the formation of meaning through their interaction, making it co-created.

- **Fluidity and constant change in communication:** The nature of communication is seen as an evolving process, where change is constant and expected.

- **Recognition of communicative barriers as part of the process:** Obstacles to effective communication are considered elements to be managed within the interaction.

- **The message is affected by perceptions and previous experiences:** Personal stories and perceptions influence how the message is transmitted and received.

- **Adaptability and flexibility in communication:** The ability to adapt messages in response to feedback and the flow of the conversation is essential.

- **Commitment and active participation of all involved:** All participants are required to be actively engaged for communication to be effective.

- **Development of relationships through communication:** The model facilitates the construction and strengthening of personal relationships by allowing more meaningful and personal interactions.

The transactional communication model is extremely convenient for understanding the complexity of human interactions in situations where communication is fluid and bi-directional; it captures the essence of how people communicate in real life, highlighting the importance of instant feedback and the role of non-verbal cues and context.

Its application can be challenging in contexts where communication must be structured or formalized, as it presupposes a level of informality and openness that is not always possible.

The Role of Listening

Listening is important in communication, acting as a complement to the act of speaking. It is more than receiving sounds, it is an active process of interpreting and understanding the other's message, showing empathy and respect for the point of view of the interlocutor. That is why effective communication depends on both the ability to express clearly and the ability to hear what is being said, because this facilitates conflict resolution, strengthens relationships, and promotes a richer exchange of ideas.

Although in chapter two I will dedicate some pages to improving listening skills, I want to leave a list of tips that you can begin to implement:

- Maintain eye contact with the speaker, showing interest and respect for what they are saying.

- Avoid interrupting while the other person is speaking; let the speaker fully express their ideas and feelings.

- Ask relevant questions that demonstrate your understanding, this helps clarify the message and shows that you are engaged in the conversation.

- Reflect and paraphrase what you have heard; this way you assure the speaker that you have understood the message correctly.

- Control your reactions and emotions.

- Observe the speaker's non-verbal language, gestures, facial expressions, and tone of voice can add meaning to the verbal message.

- Eliminate distractions and focus your attention on the speaker, deactivate electronic devices, and focus on the conversation.

- Be patient and give the speaker time to express themselves, not everyone articulates their thoughts with the same speed or clarity.

- Demonstrate empathy and understanding. To do this, try to put yourself in the other person's shoes to understand their perspective.

This focus on listening transforms communication from a simple exchange of information into an opportunity for personal growth and strengthening bonds.

Verbal vs Non-Verbal Communication

Human communication is a complex and multifaceted phenomenon, encompassing both verbal and non-verbal communication. Both forms are fundamental to understanding how we interact with each other, each with its distinctive characteristics and applications in our daily lives.

Verbal Communication

Verbal communication refers to the use of words and language to transmit messages between individuals. It can occur both orally, such as in face-to-face conversations, telephone calls, and speeches, and in written form, through letters, emails, text messages, and other written media.

These are its characteristics:

- It requires that the message be clear and understandable for the recipient.

- Verbal messages usually follow a logical structure, facilitating understanding of the content.

- The choice of precise words improves the effectiveness of the message, reducing misunderstandings.

- It allows you to adjust the message according to the audience and context.

- In face-to-face situations, it allows you to receive a direct and quick response.

- The tone of voice and inflection can significantly alter the meaning of the verbal message.

Imagine a job interview. The interviewer asks about your skills and experiences. Here, you use verbal communication to articulate your answers; carefully choosing words to present yourself in the best light possible. Confident tone and well-structured responses communicate not only information but also your enthusiasm and professionalism.

Non-Verbal Communication

Non-verbal communication includes gestures, facial expressions, postures, proxemics (use of personal space), eye contact, and other non-linguistic behaviors through which we transmit and receive messages. It often occurs unconsciously and can complement, contradict, or reinforce verbal communication.

These are its characteristics:

- Some gestures and facial expressions are universal and recognized in various cultures.

- Many aspects of non-verbal communication are done subconsciously.

- The meaning of non-verbal gestures can vary significantly depending on the cultural and situational context.

- It is especially effective for transmitting emotions.

- Complements verbal communication, adding depth and meaning to the message.

- Non-verbal signals tend to be more immediate and spontaneous than verbal language.

During the same job interview, continuing with the example I gave you at the end of the verbal communication, apart from your verbal responses, your body language is important. Maintaining eye contact demonstrates confidence, while an open, relaxed posture can indicate comfort and sincerity. These non-verbal elements reinforce the message you are trying to communicate verbally.

Differences Between Verbal and Non-Verbal Communication

While these types of communication are integral components of human interaction, there are key differences between them.

Verbal communication focuses on explicit content, words, and language structure to convey messages. It is direct, and in its oral form, it allows instant feedback, which facilitates clarification and mutual understanding.

In contrast, non-verbal communication is more concerned with transmitting the emotional context and subtleties of the message, usually unconsciously, providing clues about the sincerity, attitude, and feelings of the sender, complementing or, in some cases, contradicting what is said verbally.

Nonverbal communication can reveal intentions and emotions that words alone cannot, while verbal communication offers the structure and clarity necessary for the exchange of complex and specific ideas.

Practical Example of Verbal and Non-Verbal Communication in Human Interactions

Imagine any given Saturday, where you decide to spend the afternoon in a cafe with a friend you haven't seen in months. This familiar and everyday scenario is the perfect backdrop to explore how both types of communication complement each other.

From the moment you meet your friend, non-verbal communication begins to weave its magic.

A warm hug, accompanied by a genuine smile, immediately sets a tone of joy and comfort for the conversation that is about to begin. These simple but powerful non-verbal gestures communicate affection and anticipation without the need for words.

As you sit at a table by the window, the two of you share stories about the past few months. Here, verbal communication takes center stage. You narrate your experiences, choosing words that convey not only the facts but also your emotions; the intonation of your voice varies depending on the moment: the excitement of a recent achievement, the serenity when reflecting on difficult moments, each change in your tone brings an additional dimension to the words, enriching the story and facilitating a deeper understanding on the part of your friend.

Your body language reinforces and qualifies the verbal message. Animated gestures when sharing a funny anecdote, direct eye contact during a moment of sincerity, and leaning forward to emphasize an important point all contribute to the richness of communication.

Your friend responds in a similar way, using both verbal and non-verbal communication. They nod with understanding, their facial expressions reflect a range of emotions in response to your story, and these non-verbal reactions, along with their own stories and verbal comments, create a fluid and reciprocal dialogue.

This example illustrates the importance of integrating verbal and non-verbal communication into our daily interactions. It is not simply about what we say, but how we say it and accompany it with our body and expressions.

Communication Barriers

They are obstacles that interfere with the information exchange process, affecting the effectiveness with which messages are sent, received, and understood. They arise at any stage of the communication process and have the potential to distort the original intention of the message, leading to misunderstandings, conflicts, and, in some cases, complete failure of communication. They can be of varied nature, including linguistic, cultural, emotional, physical, and perceptual aspects.

Below, I present the details of each of these barriers and some practical tips to facilitate a more effective, and empathetic type of communication:

1. Language

It has to do with the communication difficulties that arise when the people interacting speak different languages or dialects. This barrier involves the literal translation of words and the interpretation of meanings, which can vary widely between different languages.

This leads to misunderstandings, misinterpretations, and in some cases, the inability to communicate completely.

Recommendations to overcome it:

- Learn the basic language or key phrases of the interlocutor.

- Use translation tools and applications for real-time assistance.

- Use effective non-verbal communication to complement the verbal message.

- Practice active listening to ensure understanding.

- Be patient and maintain an open attitude towards errors and corrections.

- Look for common or universal contexts to facilitate understanding.

- Use interpreters or linguistic mediators if necessary.

- Simplify the language, avoiding jargon and technical terms.

- Confirm mutual understanding through paraphrasing.

Every effort you make to cross this linguistic bridge improves your communication skills and enriches your understanding of the world.

2. Cultural Differences

Culture affects perceptions, gestures, body language, norms of courtesy, and values, all of which can influence how a message is interpreted.

Cultural differences create barriers to communication by introducing different expectations about appropriate behavior, the meaning of gestures, and how to express agreement or disagreement.

These are the recommendations to overcome this barrier:

- Be informed about the other's culture, including social and communication norms.

- Show respect for cultural differences and be open to learning from them.

- Use clear and simple language, avoiding local idioms.

- Observe and adapt to the culture's non-verbal communication norms.

- Avoid assumptions or stereotypes about culturally based behaviors.

- Demonstrate empathy and patience in the face of misunderstandings.

- Foster an environment of mutual respect and cultural curiosity.

- Be aware of one's cultural tendencies and how they can be perceived.

- Seek feedback to better understand cultural perspectives.

Accepting and adapting to cultural differences is essential in our globalized world.

3. Physical Barriers

These are more tangible or environmental obstacles that prevent or distort the effective transmission of messages between sender and receiver; this includes geographic distance, environmental noise, architectural barriers, and poor-quality media.

They cause messages to be lost or misinterpreted. For example, noise in an environment can drown out a speaker's voice, while a poor Internet connection can interrupt a video conference, affecting the flow and understanding of the conversation.

To overcome physical barriers, you can:

- Use appropriate technology to improve the quality of the connection in remote communications.

- Ensure a quiet, distraction-free environment for important conversations.

- Use visual or written means when environmental noise is unavoidable.

- Design physical spaces that facilitate communication, such as acoustically treated meeting rooms.

- Plan meetings at times and places where interruptions are minimal.

- Confirm reception and understanding of the message when there are doubts due to interruptions.

- Adjust the volume and clarity of speech according to the needs of the environment and the receiver.

- Use effective signage and inclusive design in public spaces to overcome architectural barriers.

I encourage you to consider the physical environment as a key component of successful communication, adapting and using tools at your disposal to overcome these barriers.

4. Emotional Barriers

They are those internal barriers related to feelings, emotions, and personal perceptions that can affect how we communicate and receive messages, such as fear, anxiety, lack of confidence, prejudices, and negative emotions such as anger or sadness.

For example, fear of being judged can prevent a person from sharing their true thoughts, limiting the depth and authenticity of the conversation.

To overcome these barriers, I give you the following tips:

- Recognize and accept your own emotions before starting a conversation.

- Practice relaxation or meditation techniques to reduce anxiety and stress.

- Develop self-confidence through preparation and practice in low-pressure situations.

- Strive to listen actively, showing empathy towards the feelings of the other.

- Keep an open mind, avoiding pre-judgments or premature judgments.

- Express emotions constructively, using "I feel" to communicate how certain situations affect you.

- Seek honest and constructive feedback to improve your communication.

- Work on building relationships of trust where emotional expression is valued and safe.

- Accept that vulnerability is a natural part of human relationships and can strengthen communication.

Effective communication begins with understanding and managing our own emotions, opening doors to richer and more meaningful interactions.

5. Perceptual Barriers

These are the personal predispositions, interpretations, and expectations that everyone has and that can distort how information is received and interpreted. They are formed by our previous experiences, beliefs, values, and attitudes, significantly influencing our perception of the messages received.

These barriers lead to misunderstandings and conflicts, as assumptions or prejudices cause us to misinterpret the intentions or meaning behind someone's words. For example, if we have a prior negative perception of a person, we may interpret their neutral comments as critical or hostile, even when that is not the intention.

To overcome these barriers, be sure to keep these tips in mind:

- Be aware of your perceptions and how they can affect your interpretation of information.

- Listen actively, focusing on the speaker's message without letting your prejudgments interfere.

- Check your interpretations by asking and clarifying before reacting.

- Practice empathy, trying to see the situation from the other's perspective.

- Maintain an open attitude, willing to change your perceptions based on new information.

- Avoid jumping to quick conclusions without sufficient evidence.

- Reflect on how your experiences and beliefs can influence your judgments.

- Foster a communication environment where everyone feels safe to express their points of view without fear of being misinterpreted.

By recognizing and adjusting how your perceptions influence the interpretation of messages, you open a channel for deeper understanding and a more authentic connection with others.

I hope that with these fundamentals, recommendations, advice, and all the information that I have shared with you, you are ready for the next step: mastering listening!

Keep moving forward with reading and preparing to talk to everyone with a high level of communication.

Chapter 2: Listening Mastery

Congratulations on moving forward on your path to more effective communication.

In the previous chapter, I introduced you to the fundamentals of communication, where I briefly highlighted the importance of listening in this complex process. Now, I will dedicate this chapter exclusively to addressing in detail this vital component for effective communication.

Listening goes beyond simply hearing the words; it is a key element to truly understanding others.

Consider for a moment how a conversation deteriorates when you don't pay real attention. Imagine you are discussing an important topic and, instead of listening, you are thinking about your next response. This can make the other person feel ignored and underestimated, causing misunderstandings and even conflict. This common scenario illustrates how failure to listen obstructs effective dispute resolution and can damage trust and mutual respect.

This chapter is designed to shift your approach to listening, giving you the tools necessary to cultivate active, empathetic listening.

Active Listening Techniques

These are essential tools in the art of effective communication. They foster an environment where everyone feels heard, validated, and understood, which is essential for building strong relationships, resolving conflicts, and improving collaboration in various contexts.

1. Paraphrase the Speaker's Message

This technique involves repeating what the speaker has said, using your own words. By paraphrasing, you confirm the accuracy of your understanding and allow the speaker to correct any misunderstanding immediately.

To put paraphrasing into practice, you must first listen carefully, absorbing both the speaker's words and the tone and emotion that accompany them. It is important to maintain an attitude of curiosity and openness, avoiding any premature judgment that could distort understanding.

Imagine a situation where a friend tells you about a problem at work. After listening, you could paraphrase by saying, "So, you feel like you're not being properly valued for all the effort you put into your projects, is that correct?" This act of paraphrasing shows that you are actively listening, and can clarify and deepen the conversation, encouraging your friend to share more details or correct any inaccuracies.

2. Ask Open-Ended Questions

Asking open-ended questions is another powerful technique, designed to encourage the speaker to share more information, thoughts, and feelings. Unlike closed-ended questions, which limit answers to a simple yes or no, these invite a deeper exploration of the topic under discussion.

Implementing this technique means asking questions that encourage the speaker to reflect and expand on their point of view. Start your questions with "How...?", "What...?" or "Why...?" allowing the speaker the freedom to express themselves broadly.

For example, if someone tells you about a new hobby they've taken up, instead of asking, "Do you like it?" which suggests a short answer, you could say, "What do you enjoy most about your new hobby?" This open-ended question encourages a detailed response, providing a window into the speaker's deepest feelings and thoughts, and potentially revealing aspects of their experience that a closed-ended question could not uncover.

3. Show Receptive Body Language

Receptive body language is a powerful way to communicate without words that you are fully engaged and open to what the speaker is sharing. Include gestures such as nodding your head, maintaining eye contact, and orienting your body toward the speaker. These nonverbal cues reinforce the message that you value what is being said and are actively involved in the conversation.

To effectively practice receptive body language, start by being aware of your posture: lean forward slightly as you listen, showing interest and attention; be sure to maintain moderate eye contact—too much can be intimidating, while too little can seem like disinterest. Occasional nodding and offering facial expressions that match the nature of what is being said are also ways to show empathy and understanding.

Imagine you are in a coffee shop with a friend who is sharing something important. When using receptive body language, you lean your body toward your friend, nod occasionally to indicate that you are following the conversation, and your facial expressions reflect the emotions your friend is expressing.

This set of actions communicates that you genuinely care about the conversation, encouraging your friend to open even more.

4. Avoid Interruptions While the Other Person Speaks

Interrupting someone while they are speaking can be a significant obstacle to effective communication, as it sends the message that what you have to say is more important than the speaker's message. Avoiding interruptions is therefore important to maintain an open and respectful flow of communication.

To avoid interrupting, first, cultivate patience, recognizing that people have their rhythm to express themselves.

If you feel the urge to speak, take a deep breath and remind yourself of the importance of listening completely. If you have thoughts or questions that arise while the other person is speaking, write them down if necessary, so that you can remember them without the need to cut off the conversation.

Consider a scenario where you are discussing a project with a colleague and an idea or concern arises while your colleague is speaking; instead of interrupting, you make a mental or physical note of what you want to say and wait for your colleague to finish their spot. Then, you can respectfully introduce your ideas or concerns, ensuring that you both can fully share and discuss your thoughts without feeling devalued.

5. Offer Positive Verbal Feedback, such as "I Understand" or "I See"

By using expressions like "I understand" or "I see," you validate the speaker's feelings and thoughts while fostering an environment of support and mutual understanding.

You need to show attention and sensitivity to what the other is expressing; listen with your whole being; perceive the emotions behind the words. During feedback, it is important that your comments genuinely reflect your understanding and empathy. Phrases like "I can imagine how you feel" or "That sounds like it would be challenging for you" can make a big difference in how the speaker perceives your level of engagement and understanding in the conversation.

A practical example of this technique can be seen in a conversation between friends, where one of them shares their anxiety about an upcoming important event. After listening carefully, you might respond with, "I understand this is causing you a lot of stress; it seems like a pretty intense situation." This shows that you have grasped the essence of their concern and that you are emotionally attuned to what your friend is experiencing.

In this process or development of the technique, authenticity is key. Responses should be thoughtful and personalized to the specific situation; generic responses may be perceived as disinterest.

This simple but powerful technique has the potential to transform ordinary conversations into meaningful exchanges, strengthening the fabric of our human connections.

Empathic Listening

Empathic listening radically transforms the art of communicating, allowing you to forge authentic and deep connections by completely immersing yourself in the experience of the person speaking to you.

In practice, you must be aware of avoiding certain common mistakes that can hinder effective communication. Some of these mistakes are avoided by implementing the techniques that I have presented to you in the previous segment. These mistakes are: interrupting the person speaking to you, especially to offer unsolicited advice or share similar experiences, which can make the other person feel belittled; allowing your own emotions and reactions to cloud your ability to listen objectively is also a common mistake; assuming that you understand the feelings or thoughts of the person speaking to you without verifying it can lead to misunderstandings and frustration. The inability to recognize and validate the speaker's emotions is another significant obstacle to empathic listening.

To effectively implement empathic listening, consider these specific recommendations:

- Assume that each shared experience is unique, adopting a stance of not knowing.

- Validate the speaker's emotions by expressing appreciation for their feelings.

- Use silence as a tool to allow the speaker to process and express their thoughts.

- Encourage the speaker to further explore their emotions and thoughts.

- Practice being authentic and vulnerable in your answers and questions.

- Offer emotional or cognitive reflections that show your understanding of the speaker's internal state.

- Encourage the speaker's communication with gestures that indicate your interest and attention.

- Clarify your doubts with questions that deepen your understanding without directing the conversation.

I am going to present to you how to put empathic listening into practice through an experience that you could live: Imagine that you are in a community garden and you approach a neighbor who seems agitated by a recent dispute over the use of the common space; instead of directing the conversation towards quick solutions or your own experience, you decide to listen to them with empathy, you put aside what you were doing and focus on them, inviting them to sit down and share what they feel. Through your body language and your responses, you demonstrate a complete willingness to understand their point of view. You validate their emotions without interrupting and use silence strategically to allow them to articulate their deepest thoughts. By asking questions that deepen the conversation, you help them think about possible solutions that respect the wishes of everyone in the community.

This approach allows your neighbor to feel understood while opening a path toward conflict resolution based on mutual understanding. This interaction, enriched by your ability to listen empathetically, strengthens your relationship and reaffirms your commitment to working together for the common good.

Overcoming Listening Biases and Selective Hearing

Listening biases are unconscious biases or prejudices that affect how you interpret what you hear. These biases distort your understanding of information, leading to misunderstandings or a lack of complete understanding in interactions. By being aware of these biases, you can work to overcome them and significantly improve your communication.

So that you can identify and overcome them, I present each of these biases to you:

- **Confirmation bias:** Where you pay more attention to information that confirms your existing beliefs.

- **Halo effect:** It occurs when a previous positive impression about a person influences how you interpret what they say.

- **Horn effect:** The opposite of the halo effect, where a bad first impression negatively affects your perception of subsequent messages.

- **Value bias:** Giving more importance to what someone says based on their status or social position.

- **Similarity bias:** Favoring those who you consider like you in opinions, beliefs, or interests.

- **Expectation bias:** Listening to what you expect to hear rather than what is said.

- **Reactivity bias:** Reacting excessively to certain words or topics without considering the full context.

Each of these hinders effective communication by limiting your ability to listen objectively and openly.

Selective listening, on the other hand, is the tendency to listen to only parts of a message or only what you want to hear, ignoring the rest. This form of listening can be particularly harmful to effective communication because it prevents a complete and objective understanding of the speaker's message.

Overcoming these biases and practicing selective listening are critical steps toward more effective communication. That's why I leave you some recommendations:

- Actively acknowledge your own biases before starting a conversation.

- Approach each dialogue as an opportunity to learn something new.

- Make a conscious effort to consider points of view that are opposite or different from your own.

- Practice comprehensive listening, paying attention to both verbal and non-verbal content.

- Keep an open mind, allowing new information to modify your previous perceptions.

- Reflect on how your personal experiences influence your interpretation of what you hear.

- Spend time reflecting on the conversation after its conclusion, evaluating how your biases may have affected your understanding.

- Actively seek feedback from others about how your biases and selective listening might be impacting your interactions.

- Broaden your exposure to diverse perspectives and cultures to challenge and expand your points of view.

- Use mindfulness techniques to focus on the present moment and minimize distraction by preconceived thoughts.

- Stay away from multitasking during conversations to avoid unconscious leakage of information.

- Question your first impressions and consider the possibility that they may be wrong or incomplete.

- Develop empathy by trying to feel what the other is expressing, beyond words.

- Take responsibility for your biases and commit to continuous learning and growth.

- Create an internal dialogue that reminds you of the importance of valuing all voices in a conversation.

If you decide to adopt these recommendations, you will transform your way of communicating and foster more authentic and deeper relationships. This path towards overcoming bias and selective hearing is a vital step towards genuine understanding and empathy, essential elements for a more connected and compassionate society.

Listening in the Digital Age

In the digital age, the way we communicate has undergone a profound transformation, redefining our listening skills in significant ways. The ubiquity of this type of communication, through emails, text messages, social networks, and video conferencing platforms, has greatly expanded our abilities to connect with others, regardless of physical distance. This change has also introduced new challenges that affect our ability to listen effectively.

One of the most notable impacts of digital communication on listening skills is the tendency to multitask. The ease of accessing multiple streams of information simultaneously can lead to decreased mindfulness during digital conversations. Unlike face-to-face interactions, where body language and non-verbal cues are vital in communication, digital conversations often lack these nuances, making it easier to become distracted and less likely to pay full attention to the speaker's message.

Furthermore, the textual nature of many digital media can lead to misinterpretations. Without the tone of voice, pauses, and inflections that convey emotion and emphasis in oral communication, messages can be misinterpreted, requiring a more careful and thoughtful form of "listening" when interpreting the meaning behind the written words.

Digital communication has also changed the way we perceive availability; and expectations of immediate response can create pressure, affecting our ability to process and respond thoughtfully. This expectation of immediacy can diminish the quality of our listening, as we rush to respond without spending enough time to truly consider the other's message.

To navigate the challenges of listening in the digital age, it is necessary to adopt strategies. This includes practicing mindfulness during digital conversations, taking pauses to reflect before responding, and seeking clarity when messages are unclear, as well as recognizing the importance of face-to-face conversations or phone calls when the topics are complex or emotionally charged, taking advantage of the richness of direct communication to guarantee deep mutual understanding.

By facing these challenges head-on and adapting your listening skills to the digital environment, you can significantly improve the quality of your online communications.

This conscious effort to maintain clarity, empathy, and mindfulness in all your digital interactions will allow you to navigate the vast and sometimes complicated world of digital communication more effectively.

So put into practice each of the active listening techniques, as well as empathetic listening and the recommendations to overcome listening biases and selective listening both in your face-to-face communications and in digital communications and through other means.

Chapter 3: Speak with Confidence

Speaking with confidence is a transformative tool that opens doors in practically all aspects of life.

From personal to professional interactions, the ability to express yourself clearly and confidently improves how others perceive you. It also reinforces your self-esteem and your ability to influence your environment.

Let's look for a moment at the daily situations you find yourself in presentations at work, important conversations with loved ones, or even moments when you need to defend your points of view, in each of these scenarios, speaking with confidence can make the difference between being heard and understood or going unnoticed.

This skill goes beyond simply projecting your voice or having a perfect command of language; it is a matter of genuinely connecting with your audience, whether it is one person or a large group, of sending a powerful message about your credibility and your confidence in what you are saying, which in turn can inspire confidence in others.

But what are the specific benefits of being a confident speaker?

In the professional field, it can be the key to advancing your career, persuading colleagues or clients, and leading teams effectively. In personal relationships, it allows you to communicate your needs and desires in a way that makes them more likely to be met. And in social situations, it helps you make more meaningful connections and leave a lasting impression on those around you.

In this chapter, I will guide you through the principles and techniques to develop and strengthen your ability to speak with confidence.

Articulate Thoughts Clearly

This is the first step to speaking with confidence; in fact, it is a skill that enhances all spheres of your life, from casual interactions to formal speeches in professional environments.

To begin to articulate your thoughts clearly, the first thing is to have in-depth knowledge about the topic you want to communicate. This foundation allows you to speak with authority and precision; key elements to transmit confidence. Let's say you want to convince your team to adopt a new strategy. Knowing every aspect of that strategy will allow you to present it in a way that answers questions before they are even asked, anticipating doubts and proactively addressing concerns.

The second thing, once you know about the topic to communicate, is the organization of your ideas. A thought can be exceptionally deep or innovative, but if it is presented in a confusing or disordered manner, its value is lost in the broadcast. To do this, before speaking, take a moment to mentally structure your message. What is the main point you want to communicate? How are the different subtopics related to each other? A coherent structure acts as a map for your audience, guiding them through your reasoning without getting lost in irrelevant details.

Third, keep adaptability in mind, because the way you articulate your thoughts should vary depending on your audience. Talking to experts in your field is not the same as explaining the same concept to someone with no prior knowledge of the subject. This adaptability requires you to adjust your vocabulary, the complexity of ideas, and the level of detail to ensure that your message is not only received but also understood.

An illustrative example could be explaining a complex concept like blockchain. To a group of technology experts, you could go into technical details, use specific terminology, and discuss its implications in depth. But when talking to someone with no prior knowledge of cryptocurrencies, you would simplify the explanation, use analogies, and avoid jargon to make the concept accessible.

If there is one thing, I can assure you, it is that public speaking will open doors for you in numerous situations, from arguing effectively in a debate to presenting your ideas convincingly in a business meeting or simply sharing your thoughts with friends and family in a more enriching way.

Start working on this today, and you will see how your confidence and the quality of your interactions improve.

Tips for Public Speaking

Speaking in public is a challenge for many people, and if this is your case, don't worry; I have decided to group in this segment five practical tips with which you can dominate an audience with your speech:

1. Practice Your Speech Several Times Before the Presentation

If you manage to master the content of your presentation, you reduce anxiety and improve your ability to interact with the audience, maintaining a natural and dynamic flow of communication.

To achieve this mastery, keep these steps in mind:

- Write your speech to clarify your main ideas and structure.

- Read aloud to adjust rhythm and pronunciation.

- Record your practice to analyze your performance and adjust.

- Perform rehearsals in front of friends or family to get used to having an audience.

- Adjust your content and delivery based on the feedback received and your self-assessment.

Suppose you must give a presentation on technological innovations at a seminar. You start by writing your speech, focusing on three key innovations that have transformed the industry in the last year. Then, you practice reading it aloud in your studio, paying attention to how the words flow and where you need to pause for effect.

After feeling somewhat comfortable with the material, you decide to record yourself with your smartphone. When playing the video, you notice that your tone needs variation to maintain interest and you decide to work on that; you notice that some gestures seem unnatural, so you practice more natural movements in front of the mirror.

Next, you invite a couple of friends over to your house for a test presentation. They act as your audience, providing invaluable practice for speaking in front of others. One of them suggests that you use more personal examples to illustrate technological innovations, making them more relatable.

With these tips in mind, you adjust your speech to include a brief story about how one of your innovations positively impacted a recent project. You practice this new version several times, feeling more and more confident.

On the day of the seminar, you arrive at the place with plenty of time to get settled. When you go on stage, you feel prepared and confident, ready to share your knowledge with the audience. Your exhaustive practice is reflected in the flow of your speech and the way you manage to capture and maintain the attention of your audience, resulting in a successful and rewarding presentation.

2. Know Your Audience to Adapt Your Message Effectively

Knowing your audience will help you adapt your speech in a way that resonates with them. Remember that this adaptation is part of the necessary steps to clearly articulate your speech, as I explained in the first point of this chapter.

Understanding your audience's interests, prior knowledge, and expectations allows you to personalize your presentation to maximize the impact and relevance of your message.

To put this advice into practice, keep the following steps in mind:

- Research the audience before the event to understand their context.

- Define the objectives of your presentation based on what you know about your listeners.

- Adapt the level of detail and vocabulary of your speech according to the audience.

- Include examples or case studies relevant to them.

- Prepare answers for possible questions or concerns they may have.

This time imagine that you are about to give a talk about the future of remote work to a group of entrepreneurs from small and medium-sized businesses. Before the event, you do some research on the common challenges these companies face related to remote work. You discover that many are interested in how to foster collaboration and business culture remotely.

With this knowledge, you decide to focus your presentation on practical strategies for building strong remote teams and maintaining a strong company culture. You customize your message to include specific examples of online collaboration tools and techniques to foster interaction and engagement among geographically dispersed teams.

During your presentation, you use clear and accessible language, avoiding technical jargon that may not be familiar to everyone in your audience. You also prepare a series of case studies from companies similar to your audience that have successfully implemented remote work strategies.

The result is a highly relevant and engaging talk that responds directly to your audience's concerns and needs, allowing you to connect deeply with them and offer real value through your presentation.

3. Use Visual Aids to Reinforce Your Key Points

This one is a proven method to reinforce your key points and make your presentation more memorable. Images, graphics, and videos can serve as powerful communication tools that complement your verbal message, making it easier for your audience to understand and retain information.

Consider these steps to implement it:

- Select relevant visual aids that directly complement the points you are making.

- Design your visuals so that they are simple and clear, avoiding overloading them with too much information.

- Integrate visual aids seamlessly into your speech, making sure each one has a specific purpose.

- Practice how and when you will refer to each visual during your presentation so that the transition is smooth.

- Check the operation of the technology before your presentation to avoid technical setbacks.

Let's say you're giving a presentation on the importance of sustainability in business. You decide to use a bar graph to show the positive impact of sustainable practices on the long-term profits of several leading companies in the sector, including before and after images of areas affected by unsustainable business practices versus areas revitalized thanks to environmentally conscious approaches.

For each key point of your talk, you prepare a specific slide: one to introduce the concept of sustainability, another for the impact on profits, and striking photos to show the visual effects of sustainable practices. You practice your speech several times, making sure that the moment you move to the next slide coincides exactly with the moment you introduce the next point in your talk.

On the day of the presentation, you arrive early to set up and test the projector and do a final rehearsal of how you will interact with your visual aids. Your presentation flows smoothly, and the images and graphics you have chosen effectively to highlight the key messages, making your audience understand and feel the urgency and importance of adopting sustainable practices.

4. Start with an Interesting Anecdote or Provocative Question

This is a powerful strategy to capture your audience's attention from the beginning. This approach sets the tone for the rest of your presentation and can make your message more engaging.

These are the steps to implement this advice:

- Choose an anecdote or question that is directly related to the main topic of your presentation.

- Make sure the beginning is brief but impactful, to capture attention without deviating from the main topic.

- Practice delivering your introduction so that it is natural and engaging.

- Observe the audience's reaction to your introduction to adjust the tone and focus of the rest of your presentation.

- Use the introduction as a bridge to connect to the first important point of your speech.

Now let's put ourselves in a scenario where you are going to talk about innovation in the technology sector and you decide to start your presentation with a provocative question: "Have you ever wondered what the world would be like if the technology we take for granted today had been scrapped in its conceptual phase?" This question piques your audience's curiosity and establishes a framework for discussing the importance of supporting innovation.

After posing the question, you pause dramatically to allow the audience to reflect and then share a short story about an inventor whose ideas were initially rejected but eventually changed the world. This anecdote serves as a powerful reminder that the path to innovation is full of challenges and rejections.

The combination of the opening question and the story captures the audience's attention immediately, preparing them to be more receptive to the points you are going to make about how to encourage and support innovation in the technology sector.

5. Control Your Body Language to Project Confidence and Approachability

The way you move, stand, and gesture can have a significant impact on how your message is received by your audience. Positive body language reinforces your verbal message, helps establish a connection with your audience, and makes your presentation more effective and engaging.

If you're wondering how to use body language to project confidence and approachability, keep these recommendations in mind:

- Maintain an upright, open posture. Standing straight with your shoulders back and feet slightly apart projects confidence and makes you appear more approachable.

- Use hand gestures to emphasize key points. Moving your hands naturally as you speak can help illustrate your ideas and keep your audience engaged.

- Establish eye contact with different parts of the audience. Looking into people's eyes makes you seem more credible and connected to your audience.

- Smile genuinely when appropriate. A smile can make you appear warmer and more approachable, fostering an emotional connection with your audience.

- Move with purpose. Walking slowly back and forth can be effective in keeping your audience's attention, as long as it is measured and does not distract from your message.

- Use pauses to your advantage. Pausing before important points can build anticipation; while pausing afterward allows your message to sink in.

- Modulate your tone of voice to maintain interest. Changing your intonation and the volume of your voice can help highlight important ideas and keep your audience engaged.

Now imagine that you are giving a talk about the importance of creativity in personal development. You begin your presentation by standing firmly and confidently in the center of the stage, which immediately captures your audience's attention. When introducing the topic, you use hand gestures to accompany your words, making your message more dynamic and engaging.

As you progress through your presentation, you establish eye contact with different sectors of the audience, creating a sense of inclusion and personal connection. At key moments, you smile to emphasize the joy and excitement creativity brings to our lives, making you more approachable.

When you reach a crucial point in your talk, you pause briefly, creating a dramatic pause that prepares the audience for what is to come. Then, with a voice full of conviction, you share an inspiring quote about creativity, using a tone that varies in intonation and volume to keep everyone engaged.

As you conclude, you slowly walk to the front of the stage, extending your hands in a gesture of thanks, showing your appreciation for the audience's attention. This final body language reinforces your message of openness and gratitude, leaving a lasting impression on your audience.

With practice and awareness, you can use these aspects of your non-verbal communication to complement and reinforce your verbal messages, creating memorable and meaningful experiences for your audience.

Overcome Fear and Anxiety

If when you think about speaking on a stage, in front of a group, or even with another known or unknown person, you feel fear or anxiety, then you need to consider a series of strategies.

1. Positive Visualization Technique Focused on Success

This technique consists of carefully and consciously imagining success in a future situation, such as public speaking.

It is based on the premise that your mind and body do not distinguish between imagined and real experiences, thus preparing you to act with confidence when the time comes.

It is important to reduce fear and anxiety by replacing negative thoughts with a positive expectation of success. This improves your confidence, reduces stress, and prepares you mentally to face and overcome challenges.

How to put it into practice:

- Find a quiet place where you won't be interrupted.

- Close your eyes and breathe deeply to relax.

- Imagine the scene where you are about to speak in public.

- Visualize yourself speaking with confidence and clarity.

- Observe the audience's positive reaction to your visualization.

- Focus on the details: your voice, posture, and movements.

- Imagine overcoming any unforeseen event with calm and grace.

- Visualize the end of your speech receiving applause.

- Feel the positive emotions associated with success.

- Repeat this visualization several times, especially before the event.

- Write down any positive thoughts or feelings that arise.

- Gradually return to your normal state of consciousness, maintaining a feeling of confidence.

Start today and watch how it transforms the way you approach public speaking.

2. Systematic Desensitization Through Gradual Exposure

It is a therapeutic method that consists of gradual exposure to the feared situation, in this case, public speaking, in a controlled and progressive environment, to reduce the anxiety response over time.

This technique improves your ability to handle stressful situations, increasing your confidence and reducing your general fear of public speaking.

These are the steps to put into practice this strategy to overcome fear and anxiety when speaking in public or with other people:

- Start by identifying the aspects of public speaking that make you most anxious.

- Create a ranked list of these situations, from least to most anxious.

- Develop relaxation skills that you can use during the exposure.

- Start with the situation that causes you the least anxiety, practicing in a safe environment.

- Use relaxation techniques before and during the exposure.

- Gradually, the difficulty increases by facing more anxious situations.

- Practice regularly, systematically increasing exposure.

- Reflect on each experience, noting progress and adjusting as necessary.

- Look for safe public speaking opportunities, such as small meetings or speech clubs.

- Record your feelings and progress in a journal.

- Celebrate small successes every step of the way.

Continue moving down your list until you feel a significant decrease in anxiety in situations that previously seemed overwhelming.

Don't underestimate the power of gradual exposure; it is your ladder to the freedom to express yourself without fear.

3. Application of Biofeedback to Control Physical Responses to Fear

It is a technique that uses electronic equipment to measure and obtain information in real-time about physiological processes, such as heart rate and muscle tension, allowing you to learn to control these physical responses associated with fear and anxiety.

It empowers you to take conscious control over your body's involuntary reactions, thus helping you reduce general anxiety, and improving your ability to remain calm and confident during public speaking.

To put it into practice, follow these steps:

- Investigate centers or professionals that offer bio-feedback services.

- Schedule an introductory session to familiarize yourself with the equipment and process.

- Learn to interpret the signals that the equipment provides about your physiological state.

- Practice relaxation techniques and see how they affect your physiological signals in real-time.

- Set specific goals to improve your control over these responses.

- Incorporate regular biofeedback sessions into your public speaking preparation.

- Experiment with different relaxation techniques during sessions to identify which ones are most effective for you.

- Use the knowledge you gain about your physiological responses to develop a personalized stress management plan.

- Apply these techniques before and during public speaking situations to reduce anxiety.

- Monitor your progress over time, adjusting your approach as necessary.

- Explore the integration of other stress management practices along with biofeedback.

- Commit to the process, recognizing that control over physical responses to fear is a skill that improves with practice.

This powerful tool gives you the ability to face public speaking with confidence and physiological stability.

Storytelling as a Tool

Storytelling, or the art of telling stories, is a powerful tool because it connects with listeners on an emotional level, making it easier to retain information and making your message more memorable.

To introduce it effectively, start by choosing a relevant story that connects with the topic of your speech or conversation. This story should have a clear beginning, middle, and end, and most importantly, it should include an emotional element or lesson that can be tied to the central point you want to communicate. Authenticity is key.

Imagine, for example, that you are talking about the importance of perseverance in achieving goals. Starting with a personal anecdote about a time in your life when you faced and overcame a significant challenge will capture your audience's attention and establish an emotional connection. Through storytelling, you can illustrate how perseverance played a crucial role in your success, allowing your audience to visualize the practical application of this value in their own lives.

When telling your story, pay attention to your tone of voice and body language. These should reflect the emotions of the narrative, helping your listeners immerse themselves in the experience. Pausing strategically before revealing a key moment or story conclusion can increase emotional impact and ensure that your central message is received with the importance it deserves.

Encourage your audience to reflect on how the moral of your story applies to their personal or professional context. This reinforces the message and transforms passive listeners into active participants in the communication process.

Experiment with different stories, observe your audience's reactions and adjust your approach as necessary.

Now that you have the tools to speak with confidence, it's time to delve into an aspect that I mentioned among the tips for speaking in public: body language. In the next chapter, I will be expanding on that topic.

Chapter 4: The Nuances of Body Language

In the previous chapter, I just gave you a brief explanation of the vast world of body language and its influence on communication. This element deserves closer attention, as it directly influences how you are perceived by others and how you perceive others, even without exchanging a single word, and includes your facial expressions, postures, gestures, and even the personal space you maintain when interacting with others. These nonverbals can communicate confidence, nervousness, openness, or resistance, among many other attitudes and emotions.

Deciphering Gestures and Postures

As I have already indicated, understanding gestures and postures is essential to improve your communication and strengthen your personal and professional relationships. Below, I present the guidelines to decipher and effectively use gestures and postures in your communication.

1. Open Stance vs. Closed Posture

An open posture, with arms relaxed at your sides or palms visible, suggests openness, willingness to interact, and trust. On the contrary, a closed posture, with crossed arms or shrugged shoulders, may indicate defensiveness, nervousness, or lack of interest.

- Start with your shoulders back and relax. This activity reduces tension and projects confidence.

- Keep your arms loose at your sides. Avoid crossing them so as not to appear defensive.

- Place your feet slightly apart. It stabilizes your posture and makes you appear more approachable.

- Lean your body slightly forward when someone speaks, showing interest and openness.

- Use open hand gestures when speaking to reinforce a sense of honesty and directness.

- Avoid placing objects between you and your interlocutor. This can create an invisible barrier that suggests closure.

- Modify your posture according to the interlocutor's reaction. If you notice signs of discomfort, adjust your position to appear less imposing.

- When you listen, nod occasionally. This action shows that you are open and receptive to what is being said.

Practice your open stance in front of a mirror. Make it a habit so that it feels natural in real interactions.

2. Personal Space

The distance someone maintains from you can indicate their comfort level or the relationship they have with you. A closer distance may signal trust or intimacy, while a greater distance may suggest formality or awkwardness.

Respect the personal space of others and use distance to communicate the level of formality or intimacy you wish to project. Getting too close can be seen as invasive, while staying too far away can seem distant.

Don't worry; I will cover this component of body language in communication in more detail later in this chapter when talking about proxemics.

3. Hand Gestures

Hand gestures can reinforce the message you are trying to communicate. For example, showing your palms can indicate sincerity and honesty, while pointing your finger can be perceived as aggressive.

- Start with your hands visible and relaxed. This conveys sincerity from the beginning.

- Accompany your words with gentle hand movements. This adds emphasis and clarity to your message.

- Avoid sudden or agitated gestures. They can be distracting or interpreted as nervousness.

- Use gestures to point out important ideas. This helps retain your audience's attention.

- Keep your hand movements close to your body. Too expansive can be overwhelming.

- Practice using gestures that complement your speech. This will make your communication more dynamic.

- Avoid pointing fingers. Instead, use your open hand to direct attention.

- Use your hands to show numbers or lists. This makes it easier to understand your message.

When listening, keep your hands still but visible. This shows that you are completely focused on the interlocutor.

4. Sitting Posture

The way someone sits can say a lot about their mood and interest level. Leaning forward may indicate interest and attention, while leaning back could suggest disinterest or comfort.

- Choose a chair that allows you to keep your feet on the floor. This promotes a stable and secure posture.

- Lean forward slightly. Show interest and active participation in the conversation.

- Keep your back straight. This projects confidence and professionalism.

- Avoid rocking or moving in the chair. Show patience and control.

- Use hand gestures even when sitting. Reinforce your message without being excessive.

- Cross your legs only if you can maintain a stable posture. Change positions if necessary to maintain balance.

- Maintain relaxed eye contact. Complement your open posture and your interest.

- Vary your position occasionally. This avoids rigidity and maintains energy in the conversation.

As you listen, nod, or tilt your head to show agreement or understanding. It encourages two-way communication.

5. The Use of Physical Barriers

Creating physical barriers, such as placing an object between you and another person, can be indicative of a desire for distance or discomfort.

- Keep your hands and arms at your sides or in your lap when sitting, avoiding crossing them.

- Avoid placing objects such as phones, bags, or drinks between you and the person you are talking to.

- When using electronic devices during a conversation, do it in a way that does not block your view or that of your interlocutor.

- Make sure there are no large pieces of furniture or decorative items between you and your interlocutor in a conversational setting.

- If you are at a table, try not to lean on it too much or use it as support for your arms so that it creates a barrier.

- When standing, maintain an open posture without bags or purses in front of your body.

- At meetings or dinners, choose a seat that facilitates direct visual interaction with all participants, avoiding sitting at the end of the table if possible.

- During a conversation, if you must take notes or consult documents, do so in a way that your attention remains accessible, preventing paper from acting as a barrier.

Practice self-awareness of your body language, especially in situations of stress or discomfort, to avoid inadvertently shutting down physically.

6. Leg and Foot Movement

Leg and foot movements may reveal nervousness or impatience, such as foot-swaying or finger-tapping. The direction the feet are pointing can indicate the person's object of interest.

- Keep your feet firmly on the ground. This provides a solid foundation for your posture.

- Avoid moving your feet restlessly. Show calm and control.

- Direct your feet towards your interlocutor. Indicates interest and attention.

- Avoid crossing and uncrossing your legs frequently. It may look like nervousness or impatience.

- When standing, shift your weight occasionally. This helps prevent fatigue and maintains a dynamic posture.

- Use gentle movements if you need to readjust your posture. Avoid sudden distractions.

- When sitting, avoid tapping your feet or legs. It is interpreted as boredom or anxiety.

- Practice awareness of your legs and feet. Being aware will help you better control these movements.

Use leg movement to reinforce an open stance. For example, when leaning forward to show interest, make sure your feet are positioned to support this gesture.

As you become more attentive to these details, your ability to communicate nonverbally will be enriched, improving your relationships and your ability to connect with others.

The Impact of Facial Expressions

Facial expressions are an integral part of human communication, acting as windows to our inner emotions and powerful tools for conveying messages without words.

Every raised eyebrow, smile, or frown has the power to communicate a range of feelings and reactions that words sometimes cannot fully capture.

To use facial expressions effectively in communication, you must first be aware of them. This means paying attention to how your face reflects your emotions in different situations and how these changes may be perceived by others. For example, a sincere smile, which engages the muscles around the mouth and eyes, can convey warmth and openness, inviting others to interact with you in a positive way. In contrast, a frown or a disapproving look can send signals of disagreement or disapproval, affecting the tone of the conversation.

The key to using facial expressions in your communication effectively lies in the congruence between your expressions and your words. When your facial expressions match the verbal message, you are trying to convey, you strengthen the clarity and authenticity of your communication. If you are trying to comfort someone, an expression of concern and sympathy on your face can make your words of comfort more comforting and genuine.

I am going to leave you some recommendations for using facial expressions correctly and taking advantage of this necessary element for effective communication:

- Practice facial self-awareness by observing yourself in a mirror to understand how you reflect different emotions.

- Align your facial expressions with the message you want to convey to avoid confusion and reinforce your communication.

- Use genuine smiles to create a friendly and open atmosphere that invites more fluid communication.

- Maintain soft eye contact to show interest and attention without intimidating your interlocutor.

- Use light nods and expressions of agreement to show understanding and empathy during the conversation.

- Control expressions of frustration or disagreement so as not to close communication channels and maintain an environment of respect.

- Be aware of microexpressions, those quick flashes of true emotions, to adjust your communication based on your interlocutor's actual reaction.

- Adapt your facial expressions to the cultural context of your audience to communicate respectfully and effectively.

- Observe and respond appropriately to the facial expressions of others to establish an empathetic connection and adjust your message if necessary.

- Use facial expressions of surprise or interest to show that you are fully engaged in the conversation.

- Relax your face before an important conversation to avoid inadvertently transmitting tension or nervousness.

- Modulate your expressions in professional situations to maintain a balance between seriousness and accessibility.

- Reflect on the reactions that your facial expressions may provoke in others to improve your communicative approach in future interactions.

Now, the impact of facial expressions on communication goes beyond the mere transmission of emotions. It also affects perception, impression formation, and relationship dynamics; they can act as catalysts for empathy, allowing us to feel what another person is experiencing and respond in a way that demonstrates understanding and care. This emotional exchange deepens human connections and helps in building solid and meaningful relationships.

It is important to remember that cultural context influences how facial expressions are interpreted. What is considered an expression of respect and seriousness in one culture may be seen as coldness or even hostility in another. Being aware of these differences and adapting your facial language according to the cultural context demonstrates sensitivity and respect, minimizes misunderstandings, and encourages more effective communication.

Understanding Proxemics

Previously, I mentioned and briefly explained the importance of space in our communication by exploring how to decipher gestures and postures. Now, I will delve deeper into this concept to give you a broader and more detailed understanding.

The space we maintain in our interactions is not something we choose at random; it is an integral part of how we communicate and relate to others. This is where proxemics comes into play, a term you may not use every day, but whose influence you feel in every conversation, meeting, or chance encounter.

Proxemics, coined by anthropologist Edward T. Hall in the 1960s, relates to the study of the use of space in human communication. It is how we interpret personal, social, and public space in our daily interactions. By effectively managing proxemics, you can improve comfort and connection in your interactions, avoid misunderstandings, and better adapt to diverse cultural and social contexts.

To effectively apply proxemics in your interactions, consider these recommendations:

- Observe cultural norms regarding personal space and act accordingly.

- Adjust your distance based on the relationship and context of the interaction.

- Use space to communicate the level of intimacy or formality desired.

- Be aware of how your spatial approach affects others, especially in new encounters.

- Respect the personal space of others, especially if they show signs of discomfort.

- Use physical space in meetings or presentations to emphasize points or lead attention.

- Pay attention to the layout of spaces to facilitate communication at meetings or events.

- Be flexible and adapt your use of space according to the reactions and signals of others.

- Take advantage of shared space to encourage collaboration and inclusion.

By incorporating these recommendations into your daily communication, you become more adaptive and thoughtful in your interactions. Learning to navigate and respect that space is key to talking to anyone, in any situation, effectively and respectfully.

Cultural Differences in Body Language

Each culture has its own set of norms and expectations that dictate how body language is interpreted.

Think of body language as a language without words, where every gesture, facial expression, and movement has its own meaning. As with any language, what is considered polite or respectful in one culture may be interpreted very differently in another. For example, direct eye contact is valued in many Western cultures as a sign of honesty and trust, while in some Asian or indigenous cultures, too much eye contact can be seen as defiance or disrespect.

Likewise, gestures that you consider common may have completely different meanings in other cultural contexts. A gesture as common as the thumbs up, which generally indicates approval in many countries, can be offensive in parts of the Middle East and Africa. Even the way you stand, sit, or use personal space can send unintended messages. In cultures where privacy and personal space are valued, such as in Nordic countries, maintaining too much physical closeness can be uncomfortable, while in more collectivist cultures, such as in Latin America or southern Europe, greater proximity is a sign of warmth and friendship.

So how can you address these variations to ensure effective and respectful communication?

The first step is education. Educating yourself about specific cultural norms of body language before interacting with people from different cultures can prevent misunderstandings and promote more harmonious communication.

Another step is to be observant and adaptable in your interactions. Pay attention to how people around you use their body language and respond accordingly. If you notice that your interlocutor avoids eye contact, for example, you can do the same so as not to make them uncomfortable.

Another useful strategy is to take a "when in Rome, do as the Romans" approach. In other words, try to follow the cultural practices of the place or community you are interacting with. This does not mean that you should lose your identity or feel uncomfortable with behaviors that do not align with your own values, but it does mean that you should be respectful and considerate of local customs.

Being clear about your intentions and being open to discussing cultural differences can clear up any misunderstandings that arise; most people are understanding and appreciative when they see that you are making a genuine effort to communicate respectfully.

By approaching these differences with curiosity, respect, and adaptability, you improve your ability to communicate across cultures.

Chapter 5: Creating Connections

Congratulations on reaching this key point in the book!

The goal of this chapter is to teach you how to start and maintain conversations, a skill for building strong and lasting personal and professional relationships. You will learn techniques and strategies that will equip you to face any communication situation with confidence.

The Art of Casual Chat

In chapter three I covered some techniques and tips that help you speak in public, on stage, or with groups, but what about the casual conversations, those conversations that you could have daily? Of course, I won't leave them out. I present to you five techniques to establish casual chats:

1. Use Environmental Observations to Start the Conversation

This technique is based on the idea that sharing a common experience or perception can instantly create a connection.

For example, if you're in a bookstore, you might start a conversation with someone looking at a section you're interested in by saying something like, "I noticed that you are looking at science fiction books. Do you have any recommendations? I am always looking for new readings in this genre." This type of comment shows your interest in the other and opens the door to a conversation about shared interests.

Another context could be a park where you observe someone with a dog. You might say, "Your dog seems to have a lot of energy; how do you keep them calm at home?" This demonstrates your observation and appreciation for their pet and invites you to share experiences or tips about caring for animals. Using what you see around you as a starting point for a conversation can make the beginning of the interaction more natural and less forced, establishing an atmosphere of openness and curiosity.

2. Use Humor Appropriately to Lighten the Mood

Effective humor in casual conversation is usually light and universal, avoiding controversial or personal topics that could be misinterpreted.

Now, as I did with the last technique, I will share with you several examples that will help you implement humor to start and sustain a casual conversation.

Say you experience an unexpected delay on public transportation, where you might jokingly remark, "Looks like we'll have enough time to write our memoirs before we arrive." This type of humor acknowledges the shared situation without being offensive, allowing both partners to laugh at the circumstances.

On the other hand, imagine that you are in a cafeteria and the order is taking longer than usual. You could add a touch of humor by saying something like, "Do you think they're planting the coffee now? I hope it at least comes with a story of its origin." This comment is a light way to approach waiting and invites the other person to join in on the joke, creating a moment of connection through shared laughter.

The use of humor requires a careful reading of the situation and the person you are interacting with, so observing their response will help you gauge whether you should continue along those lines or adjust your approach.

3. Find a Common Interest to Start the Conversation

This strategy is based on the idea that sharing interests can generate a more fluid and meaningful conversation. To put it into practice, start by paying attention to details that may reveal the other person's interests, which was the first technique I presented to you. And even when you find a common interest, you can also use the second technique.

If you're at a coffee shop and you see someone reading a book by an author you like, you might start the conversation with something like, "I see you're reading [name of author]. I'm fascinated by their work, especially [mention a book or specific topic]. What is your opinion about this book?" This kind of interaction creates fertile ground for a deep and enriching conversation.

Another example could be at an event or social gathering where you notice someone showing enthusiasm for a specific topic of conversation.

You could walk up and say, "I couldn't help but hear you talking about [topic of interest]. I'm really interested in that topic too. What do you think about [any specific related idea]?" This indicates that you have a genuine interest in the topic and the other person's opinion, which can lead to a lively discussion and possibly a lasting connection.

4. Praise Something Specific About the Person or Environment

Genuine praise can open people's hearts and make them more receptive to interaction, but it must be sincere and specific to avoid sounding superficial or forced. Look closely to find something you really admire or find interesting.

If you are in a social setting and notice that someone has a unique accessory or distinctive style, you could start a conversation with a compliment: "Your [accessory] is really unique. Does it have a special story behind it?" This type of comment shows that you've noticed a particular detail about the person and are interested in learning more about it, which can serve as an excellent starting point for a deeper conversation.

In a different context, such as an art exhibition or workshop, you might praise the setting, or the work being presented: "This piece of art is stunning. The way the artist has captured the emotion is incredible. What caught your attention about the exhibition?" Such a comment demonstrates your appreciation of the shared environment and encourages the other person to share their perspective.

5. Exchange Opinions on Current Topics Without Getting into Controversies

This technique involves sharing and discussing ideas about recent events or trends, providing, or proposing a common basis for meaningful interaction without triggering heated debates or uncomfortable situations.

The key to implementing this strategy successfully is choosing topics that are interesting and relevant to both of you but at the same time not divisive.

To start a conversation of this type, you can refer to a recent event or a popular trend that is of general interest, such as a technological advance, a newly released movie, or even a cultural event that is happening in your city. For example, if you are at a social gathering, you could start a dialogue by saying, "I recently read about the launch of that new space telescope and how it could change our understanding of the universe. Have you heard about it? What do you think?"

It is important to maintain an open and curious tone, avoiding confrontation. If the conversation starts to drift toward a potentially controversial topic, such as politics or religion, it's wise to gently redirect it toward a less contentious area. This keeps the atmosphere light and pleasant and allows you to get to know the other person's perspectives without putting them on the defensive.

I also recommend focusing on positive or inspiring aspects of current topics. For example, instead of discussing the political implications of a recent event, you could talk about the stories of solidarity or innovation that have emerged as a result. "I was very impressed to read about how different communities have come together to support those affected by recent natural events. It is encouraging to see so much empathy and collective action in difficult times. What recent story has inspired you?"

Each of these techniques, when used thoughtfully and authentically, can facilitate starting meaningful conversations and developing personal relationships. The key is to be genuine, show interest in the other person, and be willing to share too. By doing so, you will expand your social circle and deepen your understanding of others.

Building Connection Speed

To foster a quick and genuine connection, you must achieve two things: distinguish yourself in your interactions and generate a memorable impact.

How can you achieve those goals? In the following lines, I will explain it to you, but it is basically through the creation of shared experiences and the use of personal narratives effectively.

Creating shared experiences in real-time is a powerful way to quickly build a connection, it means looking for opportunities to experience something new together, even in everyday contexts. Let's say you are in an environment where you can experience something unique, like trying a new dish at a restaurant or playing an interactive game during an event, doing it with someone can serve as a connection accelerator. These shared experiences act as a catalyst for intimacy, as creating memories together lays a strong foundation for a long-lasting relationship.

The second thing is to use the personal narrative; something similar to what I explained to you in chapter three when talking about starting with an interesting anecdote. It's just that when it comes to casual conversations and accelerating connection with others, the key is to select stories from your life that resonate with universal emotions; challenges overcome, moments of revelation, or situations that changed your perspective. By sharing these stories, you offer insight on a deeper level and encourage the other person to empathize and connect with the underlying emotions. You could share an anecdote about a time when you faced a fear or learned something valuable from a seemingly negative experience.

When you employ these strategies, you must do so with authenticity and a genuine intention to share and connect.

Networking Strategies

Communication also aims to serve as a bridge to have contact networks; it is part of the connections for life, both in professional and social spheres. That's why I will present you with three brief but powerful strategies:

1. Attend Networking Events Specific to Your Industry

It is a tactic to expand your network of contacts. These events give you the opportunity to meet people with similar interests and objectives, and you will be able to build a network of contacts not only professionally but also socially:

- Research and select relevant events in your industry.

- Prepare a brief personal presentation or pitch.

- Bring business cards or promotional materials.

- Establish clear objectives for each event.

- Practice communication and active listening skills.

- Actively participates in discussions and sessions.

- Follow up with contacts after the event.

The key is to be proactive and maintain an open attitude to make the most of every networking opportunity.

2. Participate in Online Forums and Discussion Groups Related to Your Field

These spaces allow you to exchange ideas, with the bonus of resolving doubts and sharing knowledge with professionals from all over the world:

- Identify the most influential forums and groups in your sector, so there will be common topics and shared interests guaranteed.

- Create a professional and attractive profile.

- Regularly contribute valuable and thoughtful content.

- Ask questions and offer answers to others.

- Maintain a respectful and professional attitude.

- Look for opportunities to collaborate on projects or research.

- Expand your network by inviting connections to participate in joint projects.

It is how you establish yourself as an active and knowledgeable member of your industry, opening doors to opportunities for collaboration and professional growth that transcend geographic barriers.

3. Make Connections Through Volunteering or Community Projects

Volunteering or participating in community projects contributes positively to society, allowing you to meet people with similar values and objectives:

- Select projects that reflect your values and objectives.

- Offer your specific skills at the service of the project.

- Work as a team and build relationships with other volunteers.

- Look for feedback and ways to improve your contribution.

- Explore opportunities to meet more people within the project.

- Maintain contact with your volunteer network for future collaborations.

These activities enrich your experience and skills while connecting you with a network of passionate and committed individuals.

Deepening Personal Relationships

Now that you know how to establish connections, and even accelerate them, and create a network of contacts, I want to end this chapter by explaining how to deepen personal relationships. To do so, I will focus on very specific strategies: showing genuine interest and being a good conversation partner.

To show genuine interest, start by really focusing on the other person. To do this you must put into practice an element that I have already presented to you: actively listen to what they have to say, instead of simply waiting for your turn to speak. Pay attention to their words, what their facial expressions communicate, and their body language, which you are already equipped with the knowledge to do thanks to the previous chapters.

An effective way to demonstrate this interest is by asking questions that delve into the topics that your interlocutor finds important. For example, if someone mentions a new project they're working on, you might ask, "What excites you most about this project?" or "What are the most interesting challenges you have faced so far?" These questions show that you value their experiences and are interested in their opinions and emotions.

Be sure to remember the details people share with you and refer to them in future conversations. This shows that you listen and value what they say, strengthening the bond between the two of you. By remembering and mentioning specific details, such as the name of a project they are working on or an important event in their lives, you let them know that they are important to you.

Being a good conversation partner goes hand in hand with showing genuine interest. It involves being aware of the balance in the conversation and ensuring you both have a chance to express. Avoid monopolizing it with your own stories or points of view. Instead, seek to create a dynamic exchange where both parties feel heard and valued.

Another important aspect is to maintain a positive and open attitude, although it is natural to want to share challenges or concerns, balancing these topics with conversations about shared interests, goals, and positive experiences can make interactions more rewarding. The ability to laugh together and share moments of joy is a powerful connector that strengthens relationships.

With this chapter, the foundation for connecting with others is already built, so you're ready to learn some advanced skills. Don't stop and move on to the next chapter!

Chapter 6: Advanced Communication Skills

Now that you've mastered the basics of effective communication and are building deeper connections, you're ready to move on to more sophisticated communication skills.

Prepare to learn strategies that will give you an advantage in social and professional environments, making it easier to achieve your goals. From persuading and influencing to negotiating and resolving conflict, each skill you acquire will open new doors and allow you to navigate the world with greater confidence and effectiveness.

Persuasive Communication

Persuasive communication is a skill that allows you to influence the opinions, emotions, or behaviors of others through compelling arguments, stories, and effective presentations.

To implement persuasive communication in your daily life, consider these steps:

- Identify, clearly, your objective.

- Know your audience and what they value.

- Build your message around clear benefits for your interlocutor.

- Use data and evidence to support your points.

- Find the balance between logic and emotion in your message.

- Practice empathy to connect on a personal level.

- Be honest and maintain integrity in your arguments.

- Use stories and anecdotes to illustrate your points.

- Adapt your language to your audience's level of understanding.

- Use rhetorical questions to engage and make people think.

- Show enthusiasm and passion for your topic.

- Respect opposing opinions and be open to discussion.

- Use positive reinforcement to validate points of agreement.

- Be patient and give your audience time to process the information.

- Follow up to restate key points and offer clarification.

To explain how to implement these actions, I propose a hypothetical case in which you want to convince your team at work about adopting a new software tool that you believe will significantly improve the team's efficiency. You start by researching how this tool can address specific challenges your team currently faces, collecting data and testimonials from other users that highlight its benefits. Then, you prepare a presentation that covers the technical aspects of the tool, including real success stories and data that demonstrate its positive impact on teams similar to yours.

In the meeting with your team, you present your proposal with clarity and enthusiasm, showing how the tool can facilitate their daily work and contribute to their long-term goals. You use specific examples that connect to the team's daily tasks and highlight how each member would benefit personally. Additionally, you anticipate potential objections and prepare responses based on data and the experience of others, maintaining an open attitude to discuss any questions or concerns.

At the end of the presentation, you offer to organize a practical demonstration of the tool and commit to providing support during the adaptation process, demonstrating your commitment to the idea and to the well-being and comfort of your team.

This is how, through persuasive communication, you can effectively influence group decisions, ensuring that your ideas are considered and ultimately adopted, based on a combination of thorough preparation, presentation tailored to your audience, and thoughtful follow-up.

Negotiation Tactics

Negotiation is an important component of communication and is required in all areas of interaction. That's why I want to present you five tactics that you can implement:

1. Establish the Framework of the Negotiation from the Beginning

This tactic requires first clearly defining the objectives, expectations, and boundaries of the negotiation before getting into specific details, thereby creating a shared understanding that can guide the conversation toward mutually beneficial results.

To apply this tactic effectively, start by communicating your intentions clearly and directly. For example, in a business negotiation, this might mean establishing from the beginning what you hope to achieve and what you are willing to offer in exchange. In the context of a relationship or a conversation with friends, it could be about expressing your needs or concerns openly, establishing what you consider non-negotiable and what you are willing to compromise.

You must approach this stage of the negotiation with an attitude of openness and willingness to listen, allowing the other party to also share their framework and expectations. This demonstrates respect for their perspectives and gives you the opportunity to identify areas of common interest and potential points of agreement.

Let's say you want to plan a vacation with your partner. Starting the conversation by clearly stating your expectations about the destination, budget, and the type of activities you are interested in can help focus the discussion and avoid misunderstandings. At the same time, you invite your partner to do the same, creating a framework that will guide the search for a plan that satisfies both of you.

2. Use the Principle of Reciprocity to Encourage Mutual Concessions

The principle of reciprocity is a powerful negotiation tool that is based on the idea that people are motivated to return gestures or concessions that others make for them. In the context of negotiation, this means that by offering something of value to the other party, you increase the likelihood that they will be willing to concede something in return. This principle applies both in formal negotiations and in everyday interactions, fostering an environment of cooperation and mutual commitment.

To implement the principle of reciprocity effectively, it is crucial that concessions are perceived as genuine and not a manipulative tactic. This involves making offers that you truly believe are fair and that you believe may be of value to the other party. For example, in a business negotiation, you could offer more flexible payment terms in exchange for a long-term commitment. In personal relationships, this could translate into committing to spending more quality time together in exchange for support on a personal project.

An essential part of this tactic is effectively communicating your concessions. You need to make sure the other party clearly understands what you are offering and why. It increases the perceived value of your offer and sets a positive tone for the negotiation. A practical example on a personal level could be resolving a disagreement about household chores. You could offer to take on some of the tasks your partner usually does in exchange for their help with a specific task that you find particularly burdensome. By making an initial concession, you not only show your willingness to work together toward a solution, but you also encourage your partner to do the same, creating a positive cycle of give and take.

3. Practice Balanced Assertiveness to Defend Your Interests Without Being Aggressive

Balanced assertiveness is a crucial skill in negotiation, allowing you to defend your interests firmly while maintaining respect for the other party's needs and desires. This tactic focuses on communicating your points of view and requirements clearly and directly, without becoming passive or aggressive.

The first thing is to do internal work to identify your objectives and limits. Once you are clear about your needs, communicate them in a way that is specific and unambiguous, using language that is firm but respectful.

For example, if you are negotiating a contract and there are terms that you consider essential to your benefit, you could express your position with a phrase such as: "I understand and appreciate your point of view; however, it is essential for me to ensure [your specific need] to move forward. How can we work together to find a solution that benefits both of us?"

4. Implement Anchoring to Influence Expectations

Anchoring is a powerful technique that involves establishing a reference point or standard at the beginning of the conversation, which serves to influence perceptions and expectations during the negotiation. This anchor acts as a starting point for the discussion and can affect how the other party views subsequent proposals. To effectively use anchoring in your negotiations, start by presenting an initial proposal that is ambitious but reasonable.

For example, if you are discussing the price of a service you offer, starting the conversation with a figure that reflects the superior value of your offer can set a high benchmark. You could say: "Based on the exceptional quality and proven results our service provides, the starting price is [your anchor figure]. I am open to discussing how this service can meet your specific needs."

Conflict Management

The first step to managing conflict effectively is to adopt an open, non-defensive mindset. Recognize that conflict is not necessarily negative, and, if handled correctly, it can be an opportunity to grow and improve if correctly handled. Approaching conflict with a willingness to understand the other person's perspective and find a mutually beneficial solution is essential. This requires you to put aside your prejudices and listen actively, seeking to fully understand the other's point of view and emotions before responding.

Clear and direct communication contributes to correct and productive conflict management. Express your thoughts and feelings honestly and specifically, avoiding generalizations or accusations. For example, instead of saying, "You always ignore my opinions," try expressing your concern more precisely: "I was frustrated when my suggestion wasn't considered in yesterday's meeting." This prevents the other person from becoming defensive and encourages a more constructive dialogue.

You must approach conflict as a shared problem that requires a joint solution, rather than a fight that must be won. This requires identifying common objectives and working together toward solutions that meet the needs of both parties. During this process, be creative in searching for alternatives and willing to make concessions when appropriate.

Sometimes taking a break is beneficial, especially if emotions run high. A short break allows everyone to reflect, calm down, and consider the situation with a new perspective. By resuming the conversation, you are more likely to be able to approach the conflict in a rational and focused manner, reducing the risk of saying or doing something driven solely by emotion.

When you approach disagreements with empathy, respect, and a genuine willingness to find win-win solutions, you resolve problems more effectively, building trust and mutual respect that will strengthen your bonds in the long term.

Communication Across Cultures

I hope that with the tactics, tips, and recommendations in this chapter, you are ready to get started in advanced communication. But before closing this chapter, I want to talk to you about how to establish communication across cultures.

This one is a complex and fascinating field that challenges our ability to adapt to and understand people from backgrounds very different from our own. Each culture has its own codes, norms, and expectations when it comes to communication, which can easily lead to misunderstandings if not approached with sensitivity and knowledge. To communicate effectively in an intercultural context, you must recognize and respect these differences, adapting your messages to ensure they are received as you intend.

It is also necessary to become aware of the different communication styles—some cultures value directivity and clarity, while others prefer a more subtle and contextual approach. Understanding these differences allows you to adjust your communication style to avoid offending or confusing your interlocutor.

Ultimately, communicating across cultures enriches our lives, expanding our understanding of the world and strengthening our ability to interact with a wide range of people.

Chapter 7: Special Communication Contexts

On the fascinating path to communication mastery, you have accumulated a treasure of knowledge and skills that prepare you to face a variety of situations.

However, there are special contexts that present unique challenges and require very specific communication approaches. These scenarios demand that you apply everything you have learned adaptively and creatively, using the tools and strategies you have acquired so far in new and often more focused ways.

In this chapter, I will focus on addressing those special communication contexts, from professional environments to online interactions. Although these scenarios may seem like they demand an entirely new set of skills, you will find that the knowledge and techniques you have developed uniquely equip you to adapt and thrive in these situations as well.

I'll focus on how you can take the fundamental principles of effective communication that you already mastered and adjust them to meet the particular demands of each special context.

Professional Communication

In the professional sphere, effective communication is the cornerstone that sustains strong working relationships, facilitates collaboration, and promotes both individual and organizational success.

In this environment, your words, your tone, and your ability to listen and respond appropriately can have a significant impact on your career and the overall work environment.

Workplace communication ranges from one-on-one conversations to large group presentations, emails, video conferences, and more. In each of these formats, the way you communicate can influence how your colleagues, superiors, and subordinates perceive you.

I leave you the recommendations for effective communication in the professional context:

- Be clear and concise in your messages.

- Use language appropriate for your audience.

- Listens actively, showing genuine interest.

- Maintain eye contact in face-to-face conversations.

- Make sure your body language is open and receptive.

- Practice empathy, considering the perspectives of others.

- Respond to emails and messages promptly.

- Be assertive without being aggressive.

- Avoid excessive use of professional jargon or acronyms.

- Adapt your communication to different channels (in person, or online).

- Foster an environment where the free sharing of ideas is encouraged.

- Offer and request constructive feedback.

- Recognizes the achievements and contributions of others.

- Handle conflicts directly and respectfully.

- Be aware of cultural differences and adapt your communication as necessary.

By following these recommendations, you will be well-equipped to navigate the complex world of workplace communication, establish strong relationships that can withstand the challenges, and take advantage of the opportunities that arise.

Social Networks and Online Communication

In today's digital age, social networks and online communication have revolutionized the way we interact, both personally and professionally.

These platforms offer unprecedented opportunities to connect, share, and learn from others on a global scale. But navigating this digital landscape requires an understanding of how to communicate effectively to build and maintain positive relationships, respect privacy, and manage public perception.

The instantaneous and often public nature of online communication poses unique challenges, including the need to be aware of how our messages may be interpreted by a diverse audience.

To be successful in this environment, it is essential to adapt your communication skills to the specificities of digital platforms. To do so, keep the following recommendations in mind:

- Think before posting or sending a message, considering how your message might be received.

- Be authentic, keeping your voice and personality genuine.

- Use clear and direct language to avoid misunderstandings.

- Maintain professionalism, even in informal online environments.

- Respect the privacy of others, avoiding sharing information without consent.

- Tailor your message and tone to the specific channel and audience.

- Engage your audience with relevant and valuable content.

- Be respectful and constructive in all exchanges, avoiding unnecessary confrontations.

- Verify the veracity of the information before sharing it.

- Use images and multimedia to enrich your messages when appropriate.

- Be aware of the cultural and linguistic differences of your audience.

- Protect your personal and professional information, appropriately configuring privacy.

- Respond to comments and messages on time to encourage dialogue.

- Monitor your online presence and actively manage your reputation.

- Continuously learn about new trends and digital tools to improve your communication.

The key is to be intentional in your approach, always remembering that behind every screen there are real people, with emotions and perceptions that are influenced by how you choose to communicate.

Intercultural Communication

This one is a complex and enriching challenge in an increasingly globalized world.

In other chapters, I have mentioned interculturality and aspects to address communication correctly under these contexts; however, I want to condense the most key recommendations in this segment.

Before leaving you the recommendations, I want to emphasize that success in intercultural communication requires more than knowledge of another language or the study of gestures and non-verbal expressions specific to a culture; it requires the willingness to learn and adapt, and a commitment to empathy and respect for differences, so put the following guidelines into practice:

- Be aware of your own biases and work to overcome them.

- Practice active listening and show openness to different perspectives.

- Learn key phrases in your interlocutor's language as a sign of respect.

- Observe and adapt your body language according to cultural norms.

- Avoid jokes, idioms, and cultural references that may not be understood.

- Be patient and tolerant of misunderstandings or communication errors.

- Use simple and clear language to facilitate understanding.

- Validate your understanding and perceptions with open-ended questions.

- Be humble and willing to learn from others.

- Recognizes and celebrates differences as opportunities for mutual enrichment.

- Maintain an attitude of constant respect towards all cultures.

- Look for common ground that can serve as a basis for connection.

- Learn and respect the rules and expectations of courtesy and protocol.

- Reflect on your experiences and seek to continually improve your intercultural skills.

Every interaction is an opportunity to learn and grow, both in your ability to communicate across cultures and in your understanding of the world.

Family and Intimate Communication

Communication in the family and intimate sphere is essential to building and maintaining healthy and lasting relationships.

These contexts require a communication approach that expresses emotions, needs, and expectations clearly and compassionately. Effective communication in these areas strengthens bonds, fosters mutual understanding, and resolves conflicts constructively. Now, typically intense emotions and the closeness of relationships can make communicating effectively challenging, highlighting the need for conscious and strategic approaches.

Addressing communication in the family and intimate relationships to improve mutual understanding and support can transform relational dynamics. It requires deliberate and continuous practice where respect, empathy, and honesty act as pillars. Keep these recommendations in mind:

- Express your feelings and needs openly and honestly.

- Listen actively, showing interest and empathy for what others are saying.

- Practice patience, giving yourself and others time to talk and reflect.

- Avoid assumptions, always seeking to clarify and understand.

- Recognize and validate the emotions of others, even when you disagree.

- Use "I" instead of "you" to talk about your feelings and avoid accusations.

- Establish healthy boundaries that respect your space and that of others.

- Foster an environment where everyone feels safe to express themselves.

- Address conflicts directly, seeking solutions together.

- Dedicate quality time to communicate without distractions.

- Show appreciation and gratitude regularly.

- Be flexible and willing to adapt to changes in relationships.

- Learn to forgive and ask for forgiveness, healing wounds to move forward.

- Involve everyone in important decisions, promoting a sense of belonging.

- Celebrate achievements and happy moments together, strengthening the bond.

It's not about achieving perfection, but about constantly striving to improve the way we connect and care for each other. This collective effort to communicate more effectively is one of the most valuable gifts you can give to your loved ones and yourself.

Now, it's time to move on to common communication challenges and how to overcome them. I'll present that to you in the next chapter so don't stop now.

Chapter 8: Overcoming Common Challenges

Now, in chapter eight, I'll give you some keys to overcoming common challenges you might face in your daily interactions. Get ready to strengthen your communication skills and overcome any obstacle with confidence and expertise.

Dealing with Difficult People

Difficult people can vary widely in their behaviors, and dealing with these situations requires patience and clarity, as well as specific techniques that allow you to navigate these interactions effectively.

One tactic is to "mirror" the difficult person's behavior. It doesn't mean replicating their negativity or resistance, but rather verbalizing what you observe about their behavior neutrally and objectively. For example, if someone constantly complains or rejects suggestions without offering alternatives, you can say, "It sounds like you're not completely satisfied with the options we've considered. Do you have any specific solutions in mind?" In this way, you invite them to reflect and show that you are trying to understand their point of view without falling into a cycle of negativity.

Another strategy is the "depersonalization" of the situation. Difficult people often provoke an emotional response that makes the situation personal. By focusing on the facts and stripping the interaction of any emotional charge, you can keep the conversation more objective and focused. If someone attacks you personally during an argument, you could respond with: "I understand that this is a passionate topic; however, I think that it would be more productive to focus on the data and what we're trying to solve."

"Negotiating with a conditional yes" is another useful technique. Faced with someone who seems to oppose all proposals, instead of directly confronting their resistance, try to find conditions under which they might agree, for example, if a colleague is resistant to adopting a new process, you can ask: "Under what conditions would you consider this new proposal viable?" This action transforms the conversation from a confrontation to a search for acceptable solutions.

In situations where emotions are running high, applying a "strategic pause" can be invaluable. It means recognizing when a conversation is getting too heated and gently suggesting revisiting it later after everyone has had time to reflect. "I think it is an important topic and I would like us to approach it with a cool head. Can we continue this conversation tomorrow?"

"Positive reinforcement" of constructive behaviors is a great tool in communication with conflictive or difficult people, so when the difficult person shows even a small degree of cooperation or openness, recognize, and thank them. This recognition can motivate more positive behaviors in the future. "I appreciate you sharing your perspective. It helps to better understand your point of view."

The key is to stay focused, patient, and, above all, willing to find common ground even in the most challenging moments.

Communicating Under Pressure

In high-tension situations, such as a difficult negotiation, responding to a crisis, or handling a sensitive conversation on a personal level, the way you communicate can determine the success or failure of the interaction.

A specific technique to improve communication under pressure is "narrative control." It means taking the initiative in the conversation to guide it towards a terrain where you feel more comfortable and safer. For example, if you are faced with a series of complicated questions during a critical meeting, instead of allowing yourself to be dragged into a corner, steer the conversation back to points where you have clear and well-founded answers. This allows you to maintain control of the dialogue and avoid being overwhelmed by the situation.

Another way is through so-called "scenario preparation", which consists of, before entering a high-pressure communication situation, spending time anticipating possible questions or challenges and preparing your responses. This method is similar to training an athlete, where repetition improves skill and confidence. Imagine you're about to present a project to a group of critical stakeholders. Spending hours rehearsing your key points, anticipating their concerns, and preparing solid responses can make a big difference in your ability to handle the pressure during the actual presentation.

On the other hand, "strategic breathing and pausing" are critical tools in your arsenal for communicating under pressure.

Another recommendation I can give you is to clarify before answering because, in the heat of the moment, it is easy to misinterpret what others say or ask. Taking a moment to ask for clarification can give you valuable time to think about an appropriate response and ensure you are correctly addressing the point at hand.

Adapting to Changing Environments

Changing environments can manifest themselves in a variety of ways, such as an abrupt change in team dynamics due to the incorporation of new technologies, the need to manage a project with collaborators who are in different time zones, or even adapting to the new forms of social interaction that emerge with trends in social networks.

A specialized strategy to communicate effectively in these contexts is intelligent digital navigation, which consists of focusing on the ability to discern and select the most effective communication channels for each situation. For example, while an email may be suitable for sending a detailed project update, an instant messaging platform might be preferable for coordinating daily tasks on a remote team. The key is to understand the strengths and limitations of each medium and adapt your communication to maximize clarity and efficiency.

Managing information overload is another strategy that will be useful in this context of changing environments. In a world where everyone is constantly bombarded with data and news, being able to communicate your points concisely and attractively is essential. It could mean learning to synthesize complex information into clear, engaging visual presentations or developing the ability to highlight the most relevant aspects of your message in the first few lines of your written communication.

Consider the scenario of a company undergoing a merger or acquisition, a classic example of a changing environment. Uncertainty and rumor can proliferate quickly, affecting team morale. In this case, proactive and transparent communication becomes an invaluable tool, which involves informing about changes as they happen and offering space for questions and concerns. For example, hosting regular Q&A sessions where employees can express their concerns and get direct answers can help mitigate anxiety and foster a sense of stability.

By focusing on these specialized strategies, you can significantly improve your ability to communicate effectively, regardless of the speed at which the world around you is moving.

Overcoming Misunderstandings

Misunderstandings can result from differences in perception, uncommunicated expectations, or simply errors in the transmission of information

A common example occurs in the workplace when instructions for a project are given without sufficient clarity. It can lead to inadequate execution of tasks, frustration on both sides and ultimately loss of time and resources. In situations like these, it is vital to address the problem at the root, clarifying expectations and ensuring that everyone involved has a uniform understanding of the objectives and procedures.

Another common scenario occurs in personal relationships, where what is said is interpreted differently than what was intended. For example, a comment made to be constructive may be perceived as critical or even hurtful. In these cases, it is important to address the misunderstanding directly, expressing your original intentions and asking how the message was interpreted to understand the other person's perspective.

To overcome misunderstandings, the first step is to acknowledge that they have occurred. Ignoring them or pretending they don't exist will only make the situation worse. Once recognized, it must be approached with an open mind and a willingness to understand.

An effective strategy is to use specific examples to illustrate your point. If a message sent via email was misinterpreted, for example, you can point out exactly what part of the message was confusing and explain what you meant. It can clear up any confusion.

Implementing a verification and feedback approach is another strategy in this type of conflict, that is, misunderstandings. After you have discussed and hoped to resolve the misunderstanding, following up to check that both parties are satisfied with the resolution and truly understanding each other's perspective can prevent residual resentment.

Chapter 9: Practical Application and Exercises

You are almost at the end of the book; only one chapter separates you from the end. With this chapter, I want to present some practices and exercises that will help you further enhance your effective communication.

Daily Communication Practices

These are practices you can do daily to improve your communication:

1. Practice Speaking or Presenting Out Loud in Front of a Mirror to Improve Clarity and Confidence

Practicing in front of a mirror allows you to observe your body language and facial expressions, adjusting in real-time to improve non-verbal communication:

- Choose a topic or speech that interests you.

- Write key points or a brief outline of the content.

- Stand in front of a mirror in a quiet space.

- Start speaking slowly, focusing on clarity.

- Observe your body language and adjust to show confidence.

- Use gestures to emphasize important points.

- Practice eye contact by looking into your eyes in the mirror.

- Vary your tone of voice to maintain interest.

- Record your practice to self-evaluate later.

- Identify words or phrases that need greater clarity.

- Repeat the speech, improving the points identified.

- Work on reducing fillers.

- Gradually increase speed without losing clarity.

- Practice regularly, varying topics for greater challenge.

- Ask for feedback from friends or family when you feel ready.

2. Perform Pronunciation and Articulation Exercises Using Tongue Twisters or Reading Aloud

Tongue twisters and reading aloud are effective methods for improving diction and speaking fluency, challenging your ability to pronounce clearly under pressure:

- Select tongue twisters of different levels of difficulty.

- Start with short and simple jobs.

- Read the tongue twister slowly, focusing on each sound.

- Increase speed gradually, maintaining clarity.

- Record your practice to identify areas for improvement.

- Repeat the same tongue twister several times.

- Choose a long text to read aloud.

- Read the text paying attention to the articulation of each word.

- Work on maintaining a constant and natural rhythm.

- Use recordings to self-assess your pronunciation and fluency.

- Incorporate more complex texts as you progress.

- Try reading at different tones and speeds.

- Use mirrors to observe the shape of your mouth and tongue.

- Share your readings with others to get feedback.

- Dedicate time daily to these exercises to see continuous improvement.

3. Record Yourself Talking About a Topic for One Minute, Then Analyzing the Clarity and Structure of the Speech

This activity gives you a unique perspective on how you communicate, allowing you to evaluate and improve your clarity and discourse structure:

- Select a topic of interest.

- Write key points to guide your speech.

- Set up a device to record yourself.

- Find a quiet place without interruptions.

- Record your speech speaking for one minute.

- Play the recording and listen carefully.

- Identify moments of lack of clarity or hesitation.

- Take note of the structure and flow of your speech.

- Evaluate your body language if you have videotaped yourself.

- Pay attention to your use of fillers.

- Observe the variation in the tone of your voice.

- Reflect on how you articulate your words.

- Consider the coherence of your key points.

- Plan how to improve specific aspects.

- Repeat the exercise incorporating your improvements.

4. Exercise Active Listening in Daily Conversations, Repeating and Summarizing What the Other Person Said

I have talked to you about active listening in previous chapters. Now, with this exercise, you can improve this skill:

- Find a conversation partner.

- Focus fully on what the other person is saying.

- Avoid interrupting while the other person is speaking.

- Observe the speaker's body language.

- Maintain appropriate eye contact.

- Nod or show gestures that indicate you are following the conversation.

- Wait for a natural pause to speak.

- Repeat in your own words what you understood.

- Ask for clarification on confusing points.

- Summarize the key points of what the other person said.

- Avoid judging or giving unsolicited advice.

- Show empathy and understanding.

- Use open-ended questions to deepen the conversation.

- Practice daily in different contexts.

- Reflect on how the practice affects your interactions.

5. Dedicate Time for Meditation or Breathing Exercises, Focusing on Calm and Presence to Improve Attention During Communication

Meditation and breathing exercises are powerful tools to center your mind and body, improving your ability to be present and attentive in your communicative interactions:

- Choose a quiet and comfortable place.

- Set a timer for five to ten minutes.

- Sit in a comfortable position, keeping your back straight.

- Close your eyes to minimize distractions.

- Become aware of your breathing, noticing how the air enters and leaves.

- Slowly count to four as you inhale and to six as you exhale.

- If your mind wanders, gently redirect it to your breathing.

- Visualize calm entering your body with each inhalation.

- With each exhale, imagine releasing tension and stress.

- Gradually deepen and slow your breathing.

- At the end of the timer, take a moment to be grateful for the time spent.

- Open your eyes slowly, maintaining a feeling of calm.

- Reflect on how you feel more centered and present.

- Commit to bringing this mindfulness into your daily conversations.

- Practice this exercise daily, increasing the duration gradually.

Role-Playing Scenarios

Role-playing scenarios are practical exercises designed to simulate real communication situations in a controlled environment.

This method allows participants to explore different roles, reactions, and responses in conversations that may be challenging, conflictive, or simply important for personal or professional life.

These are the benefits of role-playing scenarios:

- Improve empathy by experiencing different perspectives.

- Increase confidence in communication skills.

- Develop conflict resolution skills.

- Allow practice of responses to difficult situations.

- Improve the ability to handle criticism and feedback.

- Encourage creativity in the search for solutions.

- Provide a safe environment to experiment and learn.

These are the steps and recommendations for carrying out role-playing scenarios:

- Identify relevant situations or conversations to practice.

- Clearly define the roles that each participant will assume.

- Develop a brief script or outline of the situation to simulate.

- Set clear goals for the exercise (e.g., improve assertiveness).

- Create a safe environment where everyone feels comfortable participating.

- Allocate time to prepare and understand each role before starting.

- Begin role-playing, keeping the interaction as realistic as possible.

- Encourage participants to explore different communication strategies.

- Keep an open mind and avoid judging others' responses.

- Use strategic pauses to reflect and adjust focus if necessary.

- At the end, conduct a round of constructive feedback among the participants.

- Discuss what you have learned and how to apply it in real situations.

- Reflect on the emotions experienced during the exercise.

- Encourage participants to share how they felt in their roles.

- Regularly repeat role-playing scenarios with different situations.

Practicing role-playing scenarios is a dynamic and effective tool to improve communication in all its facets.

Feedback and Continuous Improvement

Feedback is a pillar on your path to continuous improvement, especially in communication. Think of it as a mirror that reflects how others perceive you and how your words and actions affect the world around you.

Receiving feedback can be challenging and make you feel vulnerable, but welcoming it with an open mind and a willing heart is an act of courage that makes the difference between stagnating and progress. Consider each piece of feedback as a gift, an opportunity to adjust your course and improve. It won't always be easy to digest, but even the harshest criticism has a grain of truth, which you can use to your advantage.

Likewise, offering feedback is an art that requires sensitivity and honesty. By sharing your observations with others, you have the power to help them in their growth process. Do it from a place of respect and with a genuine desire to contribute to their development, not from destructive criticism.

This cycle of giving, receiving, and acting on feedback will transform you into a more effective communicator, leading you to a deeper understanding of yourself and how you can positively contribute to the lives of those around you.

Building a Personal Communication Plan

This plan acts as a compass, guiding you through communication challenges and helping you focus your efforts effectively.

To begin, reflect on your strengths and areas for improvement in communication. Do you have difficulty expressing your ideas clearly, or perhaps active listening is something you could improve on? Identifying these aspects is the first step to defining specific and achievable objectives.

Once you are clear about what you want to improve, set concrete goals. For example, if you are looking to be more assertive in your conversations, your goal could be to practice assertiveness techniques in specific situations each week. The important thing is that your goals are measurable and realistic, which will allow you to see progress over time.

The next step is to research and collect resources that support your learning. This may include books, workshops, online courses, or even finding a mentor to guide you through this process.

Finally, evaluate your progress on an ongoing basis and adjust your plan as necessary.

Being flexible and willing to adapt your plan will allow you to better respond to challenges and take advantage of learning opportunities that come your way.

Now continue to the last chapter!

Chapter 10: Development of Communication Throughout Life

I know I have complimented you a few times as you read along, but now I applaud you too! You have reached the final chapter, which shows you have a great commitment to yourself. You are now ready to talk to everyone!

In this chapter, I want to leave you brief but powerful guidelines to maintain good communication development throughout your life:

Establishing and Achieving Communication Objectives

Communication goals act as beacons that guide your development efforts, allowing you to focus on specific areas of improvement and measure your progress over time.

To begin setting effective communication goals, you should conduct an honest self-assessment of your current communication skills, reflect on recent situations in which communication has played an important role, and identify moments in which you felt satisfied with your interactions and those in which you think there was room for improvement.

Once you have a clear understanding of your communication skills and areas for improvement, the next step is to define specific, achievable, and relevant objectives. For example, if you find that you often struggle to express your ideas clearly and concisely in work meetings, one of your goals might be to improve the structuring of your arguments and practice elocution before important presentations. Or if you find it challenging to have deep conversations in personal relationships, you might resolve to be more open and vulnerable in your interactions with friends and family.

Achieving these goals requires dedication and practice. This could mean seeking out public speaking opportunities to gain confidence, participating in communication workshops to develop specific skills, or even setting up regular reflection sessions to evaluate your progress and adjust your methods as necessary.

The Role of Mentoring and Coaching

Mentoring and coaching are powerful tools in the process of improving communication skills.

These supportive relationships offer personalized guidance and constructive feedback, tailored to your specific needs and goals. Through mentoring, you can benefit from the wisdom and experience of someone who has navigated similar challenges and achieved goals that you aspire to achieve. Mentors provide practical advice and strategies based on their own experiences and offer emotional support, motivation, and a valuable outside perspective that can reveal blind spots in your self-assessment.

On the other hand, coaching focuses on unlocking your potential to maximize your performance. Unlike mentoring, often based on the transmission of knowledge and experience, coaching focuses more on developing and continuously improving your communication skills through practice, reflection, and challenging your current perceptions. A coach works with you to identify and overcome internal and external obstacles that impede your communicative effectiveness, helping you establish clear objectives and design an action plan to achieve them.

A fundamental aspect of mentoring and coaching is commitment to action. Through specific tasks, such as public speaking, participating in debates, or even writing and presenting reports, you are encouraged to apply what you have learned in real situations, leading to a tangible improvement in your skills.

Join Communication Groups and Communities

Joining communication groups and communities represents an enriching strategy for those seeking to improve their communication skills. These collective spaces offer a dynamic platform for practice, learning, and sharing knowledge and experiences in a mutually supportive environment.

Another significant benefit of joining communication groups and communities is access to shared resources, workshops, and activities designed specifically to strengthen communication skills. Participating in these activities gives you practical tools and motivates you to establish and pursue personal communication goals with the support of a committed group.

Embracing Continuous Learning

Embracing learning in the field of communication is recognizing that the ability to interact effectively with others is an endless journey, filled with constant opportunities for growth and improvement.

This willingness to learn allows you to adapt to changes in social and professional dynamics, enriches your relationships, facilitates the achievement of your goals, and improves your general well-being.

This idea implies always being in search of new knowledge, whether through reading, participation in courses or workshops, or simply through observation and practice in everyday interactions. Each conversation, each encounter, offers valuable lessons about how our words and actions are perceived and the effect they have on others.

By committing to constantly grow and evolve in how you express yourself and connect with others, you open doors to infinite possibilities of understanding, collaboration, and genuine relationships.

Dear Reader,

If the pages of "How to Talk to Anyone" have touched you in any way, I invite you to share your experience. Your honest review and a photo will make the story shine for other enthusiasts, guiding their choices in this vast sea of reading options. A small gesture on your part, but a beacon of value for all of us.

Thank you for your precious contribution.

SCAN HERE!

With gratitude and respect,

Rowan Beckett

Conclusion

I welcome you to a new stage of your life; one in which effective communication becomes the bridge to deeper relationships, enriching professional opportunities, and a broader understanding of the world around you.

Yes, finishing reading this book is another beginning in your life. You have acquired valuable tools, practical strategies, and a new perspective on the power of words and silence, body language, and active listening. This knowledge is now part of you, ready to be applied in every conversation, presentation, and daily interaction.

I invite you to take this learning beyond the pages of this book. Share the source of your growth with friends, family, and colleagues, encouraging them to embark on their journey toward more effective communication.

Finally, I encourage you to keep your curiosity and your commitment to continuous learning alive. Return to the chapters in this book whenever you need guidance or inspiration, whether to prepare for a specific communication challenge or simply to refresh your knowledge. Each reading will offer you new perspectives and reinforce the skills you have already begun to develop.

Made in the USA
Columbia, SC
12 October 2024

44199092R00078